AAT

Level 4

Professional Diploma in Accounting

Business Tax FA 2021

Question Bank

For assessments from September 2022 to December 2023

First edition 2021

ISBN 9781 5097 4124 3

British Library Cataloguing-in-Publication Data
A catalogue record for this book is available from the British Library

Published by

BPP Learning Media Ltd
BPP House, Aldine Place
142-144 Uxbridge Road
London W12 8AA

www.bpp.com/learningmedia

Printed in the United Kingdom

Your learning materials, published by BPP Learning Media Ltd, are printed on paper obtained from traceable, sustainable sources.

We are grateful to the AAT for permission to reproduce the practice assessment(s). The answers to the practice assessment(s) have been published by the AAT. All other answers have been prepared by BPP Learning Media Ltd.

A note about copyright

Dear Customer

What does the little © mean and why does it matter?

Your market-leading BPP books, course materials and e-learning materials do not write and update themselves. People write them on their own behalf or as employees of an organisation that invests in this activity. Copyright law protects their livelihoods. It does so by creating rights over the use of the content.

Breach of copyright is a form of theft – as well as being a criminal offence in some jurisdictions, it is potentially a serious breach of professional ethics.

With current technology, things might seem a bit hazy but, basically, without the express permission of BPP Learning Media:

- Photocopying our materials is a breach of copyright
- Scanning, ripcasting or conversion of our digital materials into different file formats, uploading them to Facebook or e-mailing them to your friends is a breach of copyright

You can, of course, sell your books, in the form in which you have bought them – once you have finished with them. (Is this fair to your fellow students? We update for a reason.) Please note the e-products are sold on a single user licence basis: we do not supply 'unlock' codes to people who have bought them secondhand.

And what about outside the UK? BPP Learning Media strives to make our materials available at prices students can afford by local printing arrangements, pricing policies and partnerships which are clearly listed on our website. A tiny minority ignore this and indulge in criminal activity by illegally photocopying our material or supporting organisations that do. If they act illegally and unethically in one area, can you really trust them?

Contents

Question and answer bank

Introduction

This is BPP Learning Media's AAT Question Bank for *Business Tax*. It is part of a suite of ground-breaking resources produced by BPP Learning Media for AAT assessments.

This Question Bank has been written in conjunction with the BPP Course Book, and has been carefully designed to enable students to practise all of the learning outcomes and assessment criteria for the units that make up *Business Tax*. It is fully up to date as at November 2021 and reflects both the AAT's qualification specification and the sample assessments provided by the AAT.

This Question Bank contains tasks corresponding to each chapter of the Course Book. Some tasks are designed for learning purposes, others are of assessment standard.

The emphasis in all tasks and assessments is on the practical application of the skills acquired.

Assessments up to December 2023 will use the rules contained in Finance Act 2021 so tasks will focus on tax rates and thresholds for the tax year 2021/22 and financial year 2021. It may be that you have to deal with other tax years at work, in which case the rates and thresholds you use will be different. This Question Bank is focused on your assessment up to December 2023.

VAT

You may find tasks throughout this Question Bank that need you to calculate or be aware of a rate of VAT. This is stated at 20% in these examples and questions.

Approaching the assessment

When you sit the assessment it is very important that you follow the on screen instructions. This means you need to carefully read the instructions, both on the introduction screens and during specific tasks.

When you access the assessment you should be presented with an introductory screen with information similar to that shown below (taken from the introductory screen from one of the AAT's AQ2022 sample assessments for *Applied Management Accounting*).

Applied Management Accounting

Assessment information

We have provided this **practice assessment** to help you familiarise yourself with our e-assessment environment. It is designed to demonstrate as many of the possible question types you may find in a live assessment. It is not designed to be used on its own to determine whether you are ready for a live assessment.

Results will not be given at the end of this assessment. Once you have clicked 'Submit assessment', you will not be able to go back and review your responses.

As you are sitting this practice assessment via the AAT website, you can review your tasks against the mark scheme available to you on the Lifelong Learning Portal.

You will also see the following Assessment information (taken from the AAT's AQ2022 sample assessments for *Business Tax*).

Assessment information

You have **2 hours** to complete this practice assessment.

- This assessment contains **11 tasks** and you should attempt to complete **every** task,
- Each task is independent. You will not need to refer to your answers to previous tasks.
- The total number of marks for this assessment is 100.
- Read every task carefully to make sure you understand what is required.
- Where the date is relevant, it is given in the task data.
- Both minus signs and brackets can be used to indicate negative numbers **unless** task instructions state otherwise.
- You must use a full stop to indicate a decimal point. For example, write 100.57 **not** 100,57 or 10057.
- You may use a comma to indicate a number in the thousands, but you don't have to. For example, 10000 and 10,000 are both acceptable.
- If your answer requires rounding, apply normal mathematical rules **unless** the task instructions say otherwise.

The actual instructions will vary depending on the subject you are studying for. It is very important you read the instructions on the introductory screen and apply them in the assessment. You don't want to lose marks when you know the correct answer just because you have not entered it in the right format.

In general, the rules set out in the AAT practice assessments for the subject you are studying for will apply in the real assessment, but you should carefully read the information on this screen again in the real assessment, just to make sure. This screen may also confirm the VAT rate used if applicable.

A full stop is needed to indicate a decimal point. We would recommend using minus signs to indicate negative numbers and leaving out the comma signs to indicate thousands, as this results in a lower number of key strokes and less margin for error when working under time pressure. Having said that, you can use whatever is easiest for you as long as you operate within the rules set out for your particular assessment.

You have to show competence throughout the assessment and you should therefore complete all of the tasks. Don't leave questions unanswered.

In some assessments, written or complex tasks may be human marked. In this case you are given a blank space or table to enter your answer into. You are told in the assessments which tasks these are (Note. There may be none if all answers are marked by the computer).

If these involve calculations, it is a good idea to decide in advance how you are going to lay out your answers to such tasks by practising answering them on a word document or excel spreadsheet, and certainly you should try all such tasks in this Question Bank and in the AAT's environment using the sample assessment.

When asked to fill in tables, or gaps, never leave any blank even if you are unsure of the answer. Fill in your best estimate.

Note that for some assessments where there is a lot of scenario information or tables of data provided (eg tax tables), you may need to access these via 'pop-ups'. Instructions will be provided on how you can bring up the necessary data during the assessment.

Finally, take note of any task specific instructions once you are in the assessment. For example you may be asked to enter a date in a certain format or to enter a number to a certain number of decimal places.

Grading

To achieve the qualification and to be awarded a grade, you must pass all three mandatory unit assessments and two optional unit assessments.

The AAT Level 4 Diploma in Professional Accounting will be awarded a grade. This grade will be based on performance across the qualification. Unit assessments are not individually graded. These assessments are given a mark that is used in calculating the overall grade.

How overall grade is determined

You will be awarded an overall qualification grade (Distinction, Merit, and Pass). If you do not achieve the qualification you will not receive a qualification certificate, and the grade will be shown as unclassified.

The raw marks of each assessment will be converted into a percentage mark and rounded up or down to the nearest whole number. This percentage mark is then weighted according to the weighting of the unit assessment within the qualification. The resulting weighted assessment percentages are combined to arrive at a percentage mark for the whole qualification.

Grade definition	Percentage threshold
Distinction	90–100%
Merit	80–89%
Pass	70–79%
Unclassified	0–69% Or failure to pass one or more assessment/s

Re-sits

The AAT Diploma In Professional Accounting is not subject to re-sit restrictions.

You should only be entered for an assessment when you are well prepared and you expect to pass the assessment.

AAT qualifications

The material in this book may support the following AAT qualifications:

AAT Diploma in Professional Accounting Level 4 and AAT Professional Diploma in Accounting at SCQF Level 8.

Supplements

From time to time we may need to publish supplementary materials to one of our titles. This can be for a variety of reasons. From a small change in the AAT unit guidance to new legislation coming into effect between editions.

You should check our supplements page regularly for anything that may affect your learning materials. All supplements are available free of charge on our supplements page on our website at:

www.bpp.com/learning-media/about/students

Improving material and removing errors

There is a constant need to update and enhance our study materials in line with both regulatory changes and new insights into the assessments.

From our team of authors BPP appoints a subject expert to update and improve these materials for each new edition.

Their updated draft is subsequently technically checked by another author and from time to time non-technically checked by a proof reader.

We are very keen to remove as many numerical errors and narrative typos as we can but given the volume of detailed information being changed in a short space of time we know that a few errors will sometimes get through our net.

We apologise in advance for any inconvenience that an error might cause. We continue to look for new ways to improve these study materials and would welcome your suggestions. If you have any comments about this book, the BPP author of this edition can be emailed at: learning media@bpp.com.

Question Bank

Chapter 1 – Tax framework

Task 1.1

Listed below are 3 different methods of operating a business.

Put a tick in the relevant column to say whether the business method is incorporated or unincorporated.

	Incorporated ✓	Unincorporated ✓
Sole trader		
Partnership		
Limited company		

Task 1.2

The profits generated by different business methods suffer different taxes.

Show which taxes are suffered by profits generated by each business method by linking the following business methods to the appropriate taxes in the right-hand boxes.

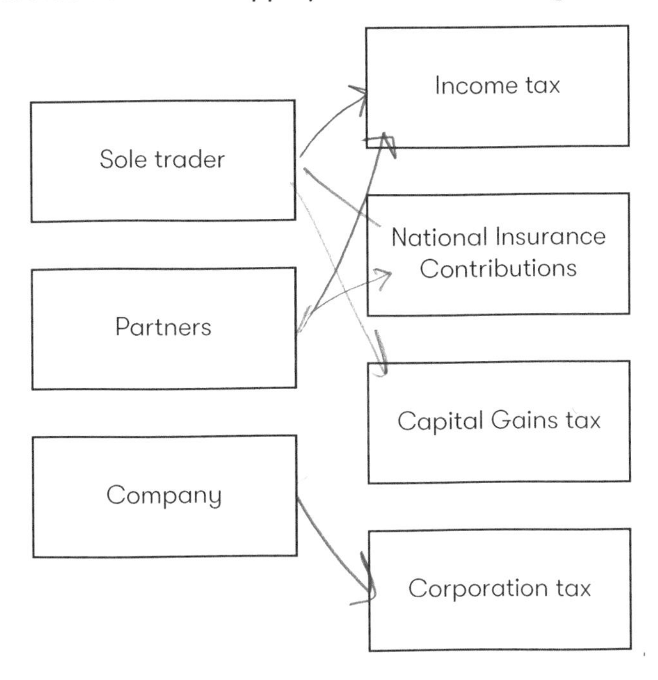

Task 1.3

Listed below are several sources of tax law and practice.

Put a tick in the relevant column to say whether the source has the force of law or not.

	Force of law ✓	No force of law ✓
Statute law	✓	
Act of Parliament	✓	
Statutory Instrument	✓	
HMRC guidance		✓
Case Law	✓	

Task 1.4

Which of the following actions by a taxpayer would not constitute tax evasion?

	✓
Claiming capital allowances on a fictitious piece of equipment	
Failing to notify HMRC of a profitable trade commenced three years ago	
Obtaining tax-free interest by investing in an ISA	✓
Deciding not to declare rental income received	

Task 1.5

List TWO ethical duties and responsibilities of an accountant.

Confidentiality Objectivity Integrity	Giving timely & constructive advice

BPP LEARNING MEDIA

Task 1.6

Tax avoidance ▼ is the use of loopholes in tax legislation to minimise tax liabilities.

Tax planning ▼ is the use of all available reliefs in the manner intended to minimise tax liabilities.

Tax evasion ▼ is the deliberate misleading of tax authorities to minimise tax liabilities.

Picklist:

avoidance
evasion
planning

Task 1.7

Jamie is employed with a salary of £60,000. He also has £10,000 of bank interest. What rate of tax will apply to his bank interest?

	✓
7.5%	
20%	
32.5%	
40%	✓

Task 1.8

Your client has deliberately understated his taxable income on his tax return. You have encouraged him to disclose this to HMRC but he has refused. Which of the following actions should you now take? Select all that apply.

	✓
Consider making a money laundering report	✓
Tell the client that you are making a money laundering report	
Cease to act for the client	✓
Advise HMRC of the omission	

Task 1.9

Are the following actions tax evasion or tax planning?

	Tax evasion ✓	Tax planning ✓
Gifting an asset to a spouse in order to reduce a capital gains tax liability		
Omitting an invoice from accounting records to push it into the following tax year		
Offering customers a discount for paying cash but not including these cash payments in the accounts or tax return		
Passing shares between spouses so that the dividend income is taxed on the spouse paying the lower rate of income tax		
Delaying the sale of an asset so that the disposal falls into the next tax year so as to utilise next year's annual exempt amount		

Task 1.10

Enid filed her income tax return for 2020/21 on 17 May 2021 and paid her income tax by the due date. However, you have just discovered that during 2020/21 Enid actually earned some extra profits, the details of which were omitted from her self-assessment tax return.

Enid has suggested that since HMRC's right to enquire into her return expired on 17 May 2022, no disclosure of the profits should be made to HMRC.

Which two of the following statements are correct about how your firm should deal with the suggestion from Enid that no disclosure is made to HMRC about the profits.

- Enid should be advised to disclose details of the profits to HMRC
- If Enid does not disclose the profits to HMRC, your firm can definitely still continue to act for her
- If your firm ceases to act for Enid, it must disclose this to JMRC and provide detailed reasons why is has ceased to act
- If Enid does not disclose the profits to HMRC, your firm would be obliged to report under the money laundering regulations

Task 1.11

Identify, by clicking on the relevant boxes in the table below, whether each of the following statements concerning tax evasion and tax avoidance is true of false.

Tax evasion is illegal	TRUE	FALSE
Both tax evasion and tax avoidance are illegal	TRUE	FALSE
Tax avoidance is legal but may fail if challenged in the courts by HMRC	TRUE	FALSE
Tax evasion always involves providing HMRC with false information	TRUE	FALSE

Task 1.12

You are a trainee accountant and your firm has a client who has refused to disclose some taxable profits to HMRC.

From an ethical viewpoint, which two of the following actions could be expected of your firm?

- Reporting under the money laundering regulations
- Advising the client to make disclosure
- Informing HMRC of the non-disclosure
- Warning the client that your firm will be reporting the non-disclosure

Task 1.13

You work for Fern LLP, a firm of accountants, which has been engaged by Ivy Ltd for many years to perform accounting and corporation tax work. Fern LLP has also just agreed to perform all the payroll functions for Ivy Ltd. In your review of Ivy Ltd's current payroll practices you have discovered that, on the instruction of the finance director, the company has recently started incorrectly paying the directors as consultants rather than employees. The amounts paid meet the definition of employment income and tax has been underpaid as a result. Ivy Ltd is a valuable client of Fern LLP, and the engagement partner is a close friend of the managing director of Ivy Ltd. The directors have made it clear that they intend to remain as consultants.

Which three fundamental ethical principles are threatened in this situation?

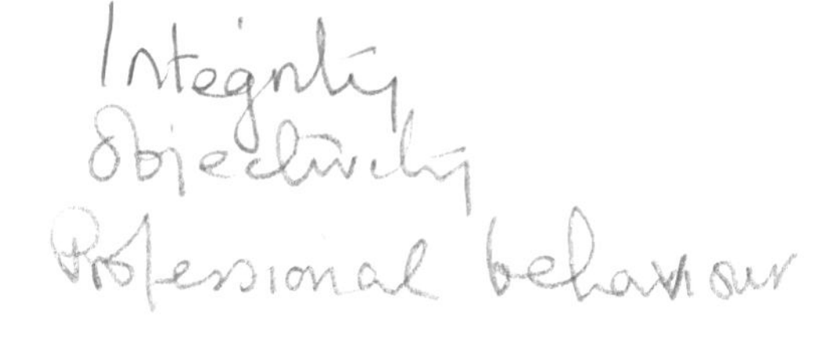

Task 1.14

You work for a firm of accountants and have received emails from two unconnected clients, extracts of which are shown below:

Spruce Ltd

'We have just received a repayment of £6,100 from HMRC. Your recent letter suggested we should be expecting £1,600. We're pretty happy about this and can now buy that extra machinery we'd been saving for.'

Liam

'I heard from Jack from your office that he's been seconded to HMRC for six months. Please ask him while he's there to look into my tax affairs and compare them to some other people's with similar income and investments, so that I can make more tax savings.'

(a) What actions should you take in response to the email from Spruce Ltd?

(b) Identify the three fundamental principles threatened if Jack does what Liam requests.

Confidentiality
Objectivity
Professional behaviour

Task 1.15

You are a trainee working for an accountancy firm. Michael is the managing director of Juniper plc, and both Michael and Juniper plc are clients of your firm.

Michael has disclosed to you that in January 2022 he set up a small business on the side of his work for Juniper plc. Michael has suggested that this new business isn't mentioned to HMRC.

Michael has stated that there may be extra work available to your firm from Juniper plc if this small business isn't mentioned to HMRC. He has reminded you that clients regularly complete client satisfaction surveys for your firm.

(a) Explain tax evasion and tax planning and which HMRC are likely to view Michael's actions are. What are the possible consequences if Michael is considered to be evading tax?

(b) Explain which fundamental principles are most threatened by Michael's comments.

Task 1.16

State whether each of the following actions by a taxpayer would constitute tax evasion?

	Tax evasion	Not tax evasion
Deciding not to declare trading income earned	✓	
Failing to notify HMRC of starting to earn rental income	✓	
Claiming capital allowances on a non-existent piece of plant or machinery	✓	

Chapter 2 – Computing trading income

Task 2.1

Harry is a sole trader. He prepares accounts for the year ended 5 April 2022 and has deducted the following items of expenditure in the statement of profit or loss:

		£
Depreciation		3,000
Accountancy fees for preparing accounts		1,000
Entertainment of:	staff (party at £300 per person for 6 employees)	1,800
	customers	2,400

How much should be added back to Harry's net profit to arrive at his adjusted taxable profit?

£	

Task 2.2

Decide how each of the following items would be treated in the tax computation of a sole trader. Tick ONE box per line.

	Allow ✓	Disallow and add back ✓	Not taxable so deduct ✓
Gifts of 30 bottles of wine to clients			
Lease costs of a car with emissions of 60g/km			
Costs of £5,000 to repair a roof			
£1,000 cost to register a patent			
Accounting profit on disposal of a van			
£500 donation to a political party			
Depreciation			

Task 2.3

The statement of profit or loss for Mr Jelly for the year ended 31 December shows:

	£		£
Staff wages	12,500	Gross profit from trading account	20,000
Light and heat	162		
Motor car expenses	350		
Postage, stationery and telephone	100		
Repairs and renewals	450		
Irrecoverable debts	238		
Miscellaneous expenses	300		
Depreciation charge	600		
Profit for the year	5,300		
	20,000		20,000

The following information is also relevant:

(1) The staff wages include £260 paid to Mr Jelly.
(2) One-seventh of the motor expenses relates to private motoring.
(3) Repairs and renewals comprise:

	£
Painting shop internally	129
Plant repairs	220
Building extension to stockroom	101
	450

(4) **Irrecoverable debt provisions**

		£			£
			Jan 1	Balances b/f	
Dec 31	Balances c/f			General	200
	General	400		Specific	360
	Specific	398			
			Dec 31	Statement of profit or loss	238
		798			798

(5) **Miscellaneous expenses include:**

	£
Donations – Oxfam	10
Advertising	115
Customer entertaining	90
Christmas gifts – ten bottles of gin and whisky	70
Legal expenses re debt collecting	15
	300

Using the proforma layout provided, compute Mr Jelly's taxable trading profit for the year ended 31 December. Input 0 (zero) if necessary, in order to fill in all unshaded boxes.

	£	£
Profit for the year per accounts		
	Add	Deduct
Staff wages		
Mr Jelly's salary		
Light and heat		
Motor expenses		
Postage, stationery and telephone		
Painting shop internally		
Plant repairs		
Stockroom extension		
Provision		
Donations		
Advertising		
Entertaining		
Gifts		
Legal expenses		
Depreciation charge		
Total net adjustments		
Taxable trading profit		

Task 2.4

Decide how each of the following items would be treated in the tax computation of a sole trader. Tick ONE box per line.

	Allow ✓	Disallow and add back ✓	Not taxable so deduct ✓
Increase in specific provision			
Decrease in general provision			
Depreciation charge			
Cocktail party held for customers			
Political donation			
Employees salary			
Repair to factory roof			

Task 2.5

Bill has trading receipts of £800. Assuming Bill makes any beneficial elections, state below what his taxable trading income will be with the different levels of expenses and whether or not he needs to make an election.

Bill	Taxable trading income	Election required? (Y/N)
Expenses of £200		
Expenses of £900		

Belinda has trading receipts of £1,500. Assuming Belinda makes any beneficial elections, state below what her taxable trading income will be with the different levels of expenses and whether or not she needs to make an election.

Belinda	Taxable trading income	Election required? (Y/N)
Expenses of £1,200		
Expenses of £300		

Task 2.6

Rohit has run his sole trade business for many years. He has calculated his profits for the year ended 31 December to be £22,000. In arriving at his accounting profits, Rohit deducted the following amounts:

(1) £900 of depreciation

(2) £800 gift aid donation to a national charity

(3) £1,000 repairs to the roof of his office building

(4) £700 legal fees in relation to a new lease over a storage unit

(5) £500 for the purchase of goods, which Rohit had taken from the business for his own use. The goods could have been sold for £600

Capital allowances for the year have been correctly calculated as £500.

Calculate taxable trading profit for Rohit's business, for the year ended 31 December, by entering adjustments to accounting profit below. If no adjustment is required, you should enter a zero. If any adjustments are deducted from accounting profits, these should be shown as a negative figure (for example, a deduction of 5,000 should be shown as -5000 or -5,000).

	£
Accounting profit	22,000
Depreciation	
Donation	
Repairs	
Legal fees	
Goods taken for own use	
Capital allowances	
Taxable profit	

Task 2.7

Tilly has run her sole trade business for many years. She has calculated her profits for the year ended 31 March to be £46,000. In arriving at his accounting profits, Tilly deducted the following amounts:

(1) £3,600 of depreciation

(2) £1,000 written off as a bad debt as a customer had gone into liquidation

(3) £60 parking fines incurred by an employee while visiting a customer

(4) £800 for a winter party entertaining clients

(5) £50 to a local charity for which Tilly received an advertisement for her business in the charity's newsletter

Capital allowances for the year have been correctly calculated as £1,000.

Calculate taxable trading profit for Tilly's business, for the year ended 31 March, by entering adjustments to accounting profit below. If no adjustment is required, you should enter a zero.

If any adjustments are deducted from accounting profits, these should be shown as a negative figure (for example, a deduction of 5,000 should be shown as -5000 or -5,000)

	£
Accounting profit	46,000
Depreciation	
Bad debt	
Parking fines	
Client entertaining	
Local charity	
Capital allowances	
Taxable profit	

Task 2.8

Identify whether the following expenses are deductible/revenue or disallowable/capital:

	Deductible/ Revenue ✓	Disallowable/ Capital ✓
Decorating office premises		
Repairs to a tractor to make it usable		
Replacing single glazed windows with double glazed equivalents		
Legal fees on renewal of a 48 year lease		
Legal fees on purchase of a 30 year lease		
Legal fees on renewal of a 60 year lease		

Task 2.9

For the following items included in calculating accounting profit, tick the correct treatment when computing the adjusted trading profits:

	No adjustment ✓	Add back ✓	Deduct ✓
Purchase of raw materials			
Private use of vehicle by an employee			
Loan to former employee written off			
Interest received on business bank account			

Task 2.10

You have been given the following information about Robbie Ltd that relates to the year ended 31 March 2022:

	£	£
Gross profit		801,220
Profit on sale of shares		45,777
Dividends received		40,500
		887,497
General expenses (note 1)	455,100	
Administrative expenses	122,010	
Wages and salaries	137,567	(714,677)
Accounting profit		172,820

Note.

1 General expenses:

These include:

	£
Qualifying charitable donation	5,000
Parking fines paid for a director	160
Depreciation	65,230
Subscription to a trade association	1,000
Donation to a political party	850

Note.

2 Capital allowances:

These have already been calculated at £38,750.

Complete the computation. If any adjustments are deducted from accounting profits, these should be shown as a negative figure (for example, a deduction of 5,000 should be shown as -5000 or -5,000). Please keep your selected answers in the same order as they appear in the picklist. (7 marks)

Accounting profit	172,820
Items added back (Picklist 1)	
▼	
▼	
▼	
▼	
Total added back	
Items deducted (Picklist 2)	
▼	
▼	
▼	
Total deducted	
Adjusted trading profits	

Picklist 1:

Qualifying charitable donation
Parking fines paid for a director
Depreciation charge
Subscription to a trade association
Donation to a political party
Administrative expenses
Wages and salaries

Picklist 2:

Profit on sale of shares
Dividends received
Administrative expenses
Wages and salaries
Capital allowances

Chapter 3 – Capital allowances

Task 3.1

For the following items of expenditure, tick if they are revenue or capital, and if they are eligible for capital allowances (and of which type):

	Revenue ✓	Capital ✓	Capital allowances - P&M	Capital allowances - SBAs
Purchase of machinery				
Rent paid for premises				
Insurance of premises				
Repairs to roof of factory				
New extension to shop				
Installation of new picture window				
Purchase of new car for owner				
Legal fees relating to purchase of new factory				
Payment of staff wages				
Accountancy costs				
Redecoration of shop				
Construction of a warehouse				

Task 3.2

Bodie, a sole trader, makes up a set of accounts for the 18 months ending 28 February 2022. The value of the general pool as at 1 September 2020 was £38,500.

His expenditure, all qualifying for capital allowances, has been as follows:

Date		£
14 January 2021	Factory machinery	1,633,333
30 March 2021	Mercedes car – CO_2 emissions 45g/km	18,000
31 March 2021	Car – CO_2 emissions 50g/km	8,000
2 June 2021	Office equipment	31,000

The Mercedes was for the proprietor's own use (20% private), while the other car was for an employee.

Machinery which had been acquired for £7,000 was sold for £3,000 on 31 December 2021 .

Complete the capital allowances computation for the period ending 28 February 2022.

You should ensure that:

- any additions qualifying for AIA and FYA are included in the appropriate column
- all allowances are included in the total allowances column
- the total allowances for the period are clearly shown
- carried forward balances are clearly shown

Any columns that are not required should be left blank.

	AIA	General pool	Private use asset	Total allowances

Task 3.3

Wolfgang commences to trade on 1 April 2021. During his first year, he incurs the following expenditure:

		£
6 May 2021	Machinery	1,050,000
6 July 2021	Car with CO_2 emissions of 0g/km	8,000
31 August 2021	Car with CO_2 emissions of 35g/km	10,500

Complete the capital allowances computation for Wolfgang the year ended 31 March 2022.

You should ensure that:

- **any additions qualifying for AIA and FYA are included in the appropriate column**
- **all allowances are included in the total allowances column**
- **the total allowances for the period are clearly shown**
- **carried forward balances are clearly shown**

Any columns that are not required should be left blank.

	AIA	FYA	General pool	Total allowances

	AIA	FYA	General pool	Total allowances

Task 3.4

Rachel is a sole trader who changed her accounting date from 31 March to 30 September with a short accounting period ending 30 September 2021.

On 1 April 2021, the brought forward balances on her plant and machinery were as follows:

	£
General pool	120,000
Car – private use 30% by Rachel	21,000
Special rate pool	17,500

She sold the car she used privately for £16,000 on 10 August 2021 and bought another car (CO_2 emissions 120g/km) on the same day for £25,000, which also had 30% private use by her.

Complete the capital allowances computation for Rachel the period ended 30 September 2021.

You should ensure that:

- any additions qualifying for AIA and FYA are included in the appropriate column
- all allowances are included in the total allowances column
- the total allowances for the period are clearly shown
- carried forward balances are clearly shown

Any columns that are not required should be left blank.

	General pool	Private use asset 1	Special rate pool	Private use asset 2	Total allowances

	General pool	Private use asset 1	Special rate pool	Private use asset 2	Total allowances

Task 3.5

At 1 March 2021 the tax written down value of Green Ltd's plant and machinery general pool was £106,000.

On 1 January 2022 a car costing £14,000 was acquired. The CO_2 emissions of the car were 70 g/km, and was used privately 30% of the time by the Finance Director. This replaced a zero emission car which was also used by the finance director. The zero emission car was sold for £3,000.

In addition, on 1 February 2022 Green Ltd had purchased new machinery for £32,000.

Complete the capital allowance computation for Green Ltd the year ended 28 February 2022. The brought forward figure at 1 March 2021 has already been entered.

You should ensure that:

- **any additions qualifying for AIA, FYA or super-deduction are included in the appropriate column**
- **all allowances are included in the total allowances column**
- **the total allowances for the period are clearly shown**
- **carried forward balances are clearly shown**

Any columns that are not required should be left blank.

	AIA	FYA	Super deduction	General pool	Special rate pool	Private use asset	Total allowances
TWDV brought forward at 1/3/21				106,000			

Task 3.6

Davies Ltd prepares accounts annually to 31 March.

During the accounting period ended 31 March 2022, Davies Ltd purchased and disposed of the following items of plant and machinery.

		£
Purchases		
10 May 2021	A second hand machine	1,260,000
16 August 2021	A car	
	(CO_2 emissions 79g/km)	22,000
12 December 2021	Computer	12,000
Disposals		
10 June 2021	A laser cutting machine, originally purchased in June 2020 for £17,500 was sold.	12,000

The tax written down value of the general pool on 1 April 2021 was £180,000.

Complete the capital allowances computation for Davies Ltd the year ended 31 March 2022.

You should ensure that:

- any additions qualifying for AIA, FYA or super-deduction are included in the appropriate column
- all allowances are included in the total allowances column
- the total allowances for the period are clearly shown
- carried forward balances are clearly shown

Any columns that are not required should be left blank.

	FYA	AIA	Super deduction	General pool	Special rate pool	Allowances

Task 3.7

XYZ plc had the following transactions in plant and machinery for the nine-month period ended 31 March 2022:

		£
Purchases		
10 July 2021	A machine	75,000
16 August 2021	A BMW with CO_2 emissions of 48g/km used privately by an employee 20% of his time	19,000
1 January 2022	An Audi with CO_2 emissions of 70g/km	25,000
Disposals		
10 January 2022	A machine, which had originally cost £8,500, was sold for £6,600.	6,600

The tax written down value of the general pool on 1 July 2021 was £230,000.

Complete the capital allowances computation for XYZ plc the period ended 31 March 2022.

You should ensure that:

- any additions qualifying for AIA, FYA or super-deduction are included in the appropriate column
- all allowances are included in the total allowances column
- the total allowances for the period are clearly shown
- carried forward balances are clearly shown

Any columns that are not required should be left blank.

	AIA	FYA	Super deduction	General pool	Special rate pool	Private use asset	Allowances

Task 3.8

Jav is a sole trader who draws up accounts to 31 March each year. Jav bought a plot of land on 1 July 2021 for £750,000. He built a factory on the land during 2021, and the costs of construction were £450,000. The building work finished on 31 December 2021, and Jav started to use the factory for the purposes of his trade on 1 February 2022.

Jav sold the factory to Sarah on 1 October 2024 for £3,000,000. Sarah is also a sole trader and draws up accounts to 31 December.

Show the SBA available to Jav and Sarah for the following accounting periods.

Jay

Accounting period	SBA
y/e 31 March 2022	
y/e 31 March 2023	
y/e 31 March 2024	
y/e 31 March 2025	

Sarah

Accounting period	SBA
y/e 31 December 2024	
y/e 31 December 2025	

Task 3.9

Which of the following costs will qualify for the Structures and Buildings Allowance (SBA)

	SBA ✓
Purchase of a factory in Nottingham from a sole trader for £800,000. The factory was constructed in 2000.	
Purchase of a newly constructed storage warehouse from a developer for £3m	
Purchase of a brownfield site for £1m to build a new factory on	
Stamp Duty Land Tax on the cost of a newly built factory	
Construction costs of a new office block	

Task 3.10

Mustafa has been trading for many years, making up accounts to 31 March.

His capital allowances tax written down values brought forward at 1 April 2021 were as follows:

General pool	£13,291
Car for Mustafa, 30% private usage	£8,745

The following capital transactions were made in the period:

		£
Additions		
10.04.21	Plant and machinery	258,100
15.04.21	Car for Mustafa, zero CO_2 emissions , 40% private usage	24,500
22.06.21	Plant and machinery	983,750

		£
Disposal		
15.04.21	Mustafa's previous car (original cost £18,000)	8,000
3.05.21	Plant and machinery (original cost £4,100)	5,970

Complete the capital allowance computation for the year ended 31 March 2022. The brought forward figures at 1 April 2021 have already been entered.

You should ensure that:

- any additions qualifying for AIA or FYA are included in the appropriate column
- all allowances are included in the total allowances column
- the total allowances for the period are clearly shown
- carried forward balances are clearly shown

Any columns that are not required should be left blank.

	FYA	AIA	General pool	Private use asset 1	Private use asset 2	Total allowances

Chapter 4 – Taxing unincorporated businesses

Task 4.1

Rachel commenced in business as a fashion designer on 1 January 2020, and made up her first accounts to 30 April 2021. Her profit for the period, adjusted for taxation, was £33,000.

Her first tax year is:

Her taxable profits in her first tax year of trading are:

£

Her taxable profits in her second tax year of trading are:

£

Her taxable profits in her third tax year of trading are:

£

Overlap profits are:

£

Task 4.2

Mr Phone commenced trading on 1 July 2019 making up accounts to 31 May each year.

Profits are:

	£
1 July 2019 to 31 May 2020	22,000
Year ended 31 May 2021	18,000
Year ended 31 May 2022	30,000

Mr Phone's basis period for 2019/20 runs from: (insert the date as xx/xx/xxxx)

to:

Mr Phone's basis period for 2020/21 runs from: (insert the date as xx/xx/xxxx)

to:

His taxable profits in his second tax year of trading are:

£	

Overlap profits are:

£	

Task 4.3

Mr Mug ceased trading on 31 December 2021. His overlap profits brought forward amount to £9,000. His profits for the last few periods of account were:

	£
Year ended 30 April 2019	36,000
Year ended 30 April 2020	48,000
Year ended 30 April 2021	16,000
Eight months ended 31 December 2021	4,000

Mr Mug's final tax year is: (insert as xxxx/xx)

Mr Mug's penultimate tax year is: (insert as xxxx/xx)

His taxable profits in his final tax year of trading are:

£	

Task 4.4

Jackie Smith started her picture framing business on 1 May 2017. Due to falling profits she ceased to trade on 29 February 2022.

Her profits for the whole period of trading were as follows.

	£
1 May 2017 – 31 July 2018	18,000
1 August 2018 – 31 July 2019	11,700
1 August 2019 – 31 July 2020	8,640
1 August 2020 – 31 July 2021	4,800
1 August 2021 – 29 February 2022	5,100

Jackie's first tax year is: (insert as xxxx/xx)

Her taxable profits in her first tax year of trading are:

£	

Jackie's second tax year is: (insert as xxxx/xx)

Her taxable profits in her second tax year of trading are:

£	

Jackie's final tax year is: (insert as xxxx/xx)

Her taxable profits in her final tax year of trading are:

£	

Over the life of her business Jackie is assessed on total profits of:

£	

Task 4.5

In each case, choose the most beneficial accounting date for the individual

	31 March ✓	30 April ✓
Harry is just starting his business and is expecting large profits initially. He would like to avoid overlap profits.		
Javier is having some cash flow problems and would like the maximum possible time to pay his tax.		

Task 4.6

Alexandra started in business as a sole trader on 1 August 2020 and prepared her first set of accounts to 30 April 2022.

Match the start date and the end date of Alexandra's basis period for the tax year 2021/22, her second tax year of trading.

1 August 2020	6 April 2021	1 May 2021
31 July 2021	5 April 2022	30 April 2022

Start date	
End date	

QUESTIONS

Task 4.7

Timothy started in business as a sole trader on 1 February 2020. He prepared his first set of accounts to 30 November 2020 and his second set of accounts to 30 November 2021. His taxable trading profits were as follows:

p/e 30 November 2020 £30,000

y/e 30 November 2021 £42,000

What are Timothy's overlap profits?

£	

(2 marks)

Task 4.8

Walter had been in business as a sole trader for many years preparing accounts to 31 December each year. He ceased trading on 31 March 2022. Walter had unrelieved overlap profits of £2,000 from commencement. His taxable trading profits were as follows:

y/e 31 December 2021	£18,000
p/e 31 March 2022	£3,000

What is Walter's taxable trading income for the final tax year of trading?

£	

Chapter 5 – Partnerships

Task 5.1

Fimbo and Florrie commenced in partnership on 1 January 2020. They produce accounts to 31 December each year and their profits have been as follows:

	Taxable profit £
Year ended 31 December 2020	10,000
Year ended 31 December 2021	20,000
Year ended 31 December 2022	25,000

Until 31 December 2021 Fimbo took 60% of the profits after receiving a £5,000 salary. Florrie took the remaining 40% of profits.

On 1 January 2022, Fimbo and Florrie invite Pom to join the partnership. It is agreed that Fimbo's salary will increase to £6,500 and the profits will then be split equally between the three partners.

Using the proforma layout provided, show the division of profit for the three periods of account. Fill in all unshaded boxes. Insert a 0 (zero) if necessary.

	Total £	Fimbo £	Florrie £	Pom £
12 months to 31 December 2020				
Salary				
Share of profits				
Total for year				
12 months to 31 December 2021				
Salary				
Share of profits				
Total for year				
12 months to 31 December 2022				
Salary				
Share of profits				
Total for year				

QUESTIONS

Task 5.2

John, Paul and George began to trade as partners on 1 January 2019. The profits of the partnership are shared in the ratio 4:3:3. The accounts for recent periods have shown the following results:

	£
Period to 31 July 2019	24,300
Year to 31 July 2020	16,200
Year to 31 July 2021	14,900

(a) **Using the proforma layout provided, show the allocation of trading profits for all three periods of account. Fill in all unshaded boxes. Insert a 0 (zero) if necessary.**

	Total £	John £	Paul £	George £
Period ended 31 July 2019				
Division of profits				
Year ended 31 July 2020				
Division of profits				
Year ended 31 July 2021				
Division of profits				

(b) **Using the proforma layout provided, calculate the taxable trading profits of John, Paul and George for all tax years. Fill in all boxes.**

	John £	Paul £	George £
2018/19			
2019/20			
2020/21			
2021/22			

Task 5.3

Strange and his partners Pavin and Lehman had traded for many years. Strange had contributed £20,000 to the business and Pavin £10,000.

Profits were shared in the ratio of 3:2:1 after providing Strange and Pavin with salaries of £15,000 and £5,000 and interest on capital of 5%.

On 1 August 2021 the profit sharing arrangements were changed to 2:2:1 after providing only Strange with a salary of £20,000, and no further interest on capital for any of the partners.

The partnership profit for the year to 31 December 2021 was £48,000.

Using the proforma layout provided, show the allocation of profit for the year to 31 December 2021. Fill in all unshaded boxes. Insert a 0 (zero) if necessary.

Year ended 31 December 2021	Total £	Strange £	Pavin £	Lehman £
To 31 July 2021				
Salaries				
Interest on capital				
Division of profits				
To 31 December 2021				
Salary				
Division of profits				
Total for year ended 31 December 2021				

Task 5.4

Bob, Annie and John started their partnership on 1 June 2012 and make accounts up to 31 May each year. The accounts have always shown taxable profits.

For the period up to 31 January 2021 each partner received a salary of £15,000 per annum and the remaining profits were shared 50% to Bob and 25% each to Annie and John. There was no interest on capital.

Bob left the partnership on 1 February 2021. The profit sharing ratio, after the same salaries, changed to 50% each to Annie and John.

Profits for the year ending 31 May 2021 were £90,000.

Using the proforma layout provided, calculate each partner's share of the profits for the year to 31 May 2021. Fill in all unshaded boxes. Insert a 0 (zero) if necessary.

Year ended 31 May 2021	Total £	Bob £	Annie £	John £
To 31 January 2021				
Salaries				
Division of profits				
To 31 May 2021				
Salaries				
Division of profits				
Total for year ended 31 May 2021				

QUESTIONS

Task 5.5

Peter and Jane have been in partnership for many years preparing accounts to 31 July each year and sharing profits equally. On 1 September 2020, they changed their profit sharing agreement so that Peter was entitled to a salary of £9,000 each year and the remaining profits were then split two parts to Peter and three parts to Jane. The partnership made a trading profit of £96,000 in the year to 31 July 2021.

What is Peter's taxable trading profit for the tax year 2021/22?

£	

Task 5.6

Robin and Stuart had been in partnership for many years preparing accounts to 31 December each year and sharing profits equally. On 1 January 2022, Tania joined the partnership and profits were then split 2:2:1. The partnership made a profit of £96,000 in the year to 31 December 2021 and £112,000 in the year to 31 December 2022.

Match the taxable trading profits of the partners for 2021/22.

£5,600	£11,200	£22,400
£47,200	£48,000	

Robin and Stuart each	
Tania	

Chapter 6 – National insurance

Task 6.1

Abraham has trading profits of £12,830 for the year ended 31 December 2021. State your answer to the nearest penny.

The Class 2 NIC liability for 2021/22 is:

£		.	

The Class 4 NIC liability for 2021/22 is:

£		.	

The total NIC liability for 2021/22 is:

£		.	

Task 6.2

John has profits of £58,000 for the year ended 31 March 2022. State your answer to the nearest penny.

The Class 2 NIC liability for 2021/22 is:

£		.	

The Class 4 NIC liability for 2021/22 is:

£		.	

The total NIC liability for 2021/22 is:

£		.	

Task 6.3

Raj has trading profits of £3,500 for 2021/22. State your answer to the nearest penny.

The Class 2 NIC liability for 2021/22 is:

£		.	

The Class 4 NIC liability for 2021/22 is:

£		.	

The total NIC liability for 2021/22 is:

£		.	

Task 6.4

Zoë is a self employed author who starts in business on 6 April 2021. In the year to 5 April 2022 she had taxable trading profits of £80,000. State your answer to the nearest penny.**The Class 2 NIC liability for 2021/22 is:**

£		.	

The Class 4 NIC liability for 2021/22 is:

£		.	

The total NIC liability for 2021/22 is:

£		.	

Task 6.5

Wendy and Jayne have been in partnership as interior designers for many years, trading as Dramatic Decors.

On 1 January 2022, Wendy and Jayne admitted Paula to the partnership. From that date, partnership profits were shared 40% to each of Wendy and Jayne and 20% to Paula. The partnership continued to make up its accounts to 31 December and the trading profit for the year to 31 December 2022 was £280,000.

Paula had not worked for many years prior to becoming a partner in Dramatic Decors.

(a) **The share of profits taxable on Paula for 2021/22 is:**

£	

and for 2022/23 is:

£	

and the overlap profits to carry forward are:

£	

(b) **The Class 4 NIC payable by Paula for 2021/22 are:**

£		.	

Task 6.6

Millie has assessable trading profits from her sole trader business of £62,000 in 2021/22. She also has income from employment of £16,000.

Calculate Millie's class 4 National Insurance Contributions by completing the table below. State your answer to the nearest penny.

Class 4 NICs	£
Class 4 NICs at 9%	
Class 4 NICs at 2%	
Total Class 4 NICs due	AUTOSUM

Task 6.7

Sheenagh started in business on 1 January 2022 as a sole trader and prepared her first set of accounts for the 14 weeks to 5 April 2022. Her taxable trading profit for that period was £10,600.

What are Sheenagh's total national insurance contributions for the tax year 2021/22?

£	

Task 6.8

Faith has been trading for a number of years. Her tax adjusted trading profit for the year ended 31 May 2021 was £53,150 and for the year ended 31 May 2022 was £50,350.

What is the amount of class 4 national insurance contributions (NIC) payable by Faith for the tax year 2021/22?

- ○ £3,674
- ○ £3,922
- ○ £3,663
- ○ £3,721

Task 6.9

Sid has been a sole trader since 2012, preparing accounts to 30 June each year. In the year to 30 June 2021 he had trading profits of £60,000 and in the year to 30 June 2022 he had trading profits of £66,000.

What is the amount of Class 4 National Insurance Contributions (NIC) that Sid will have to pay for the tax year 2021/22?

£	

Chapter 7 – Computing corporation tax

Task 7.1

Geronimo Ltd's summarised statement of profit or loss for the year ended 31 March 2022 is as follows:

	£	£
Gross profit		925,940
Operating expenses		
Depreciation charge	83,420	
Gifts (note 1)	2,800	
Professional fees (note 2)	14,900	
Repairs and renewals (note 3)	42,310	
Other expenses (all allowable)	166,030	
		(309,460)
Operating profit		616,480
Income from investments		
Debenture interest (note 4)	24,700	
Bank interest (note 4)	4,800	
Dividends (note 5)	56,000	
		85,500
		701,980
Interest payable on loans for trading purposes		(45,000)
Profit for the year before taxation		656,980

Notes

1 Gifts

Gifts are as follows:

	£
Qualifying charitable donation	1,900
Gifts to customers (food hampers costing £30 each)	900
	2,800

2 Professional fees

Professional fees are as follows:

	£
Accountancy and audit fee	4,100
Legal fees in connection with the renewal of a 20-year property lease	2,400
Legal fees in connection with the issue of a debenture loan for trade purposes	8,400
	14,900

3 Repairs and renewals

The figure of £42,310 for repairs includes £6,200 for replacing part of a wall that was knocked down by a lorry, and £12,200 for initial repairs to an office building that was acquired during the year ended 31 March 2021. The office building was not usable until the repairs were carried out, and this fact was represented by a reduced purchase price.

4 Bank interest

The bank interest and the debenture interest were both received on non-trade investments.

5 Dividends received

The dividends were received from other companies. The figure of £56,000 is the actual amount received.

6 Capital allowances

Capital allowances for the year have been calculated as £13,200.

Using the proforma layout provided, calculate Geronimo Ltd's taxable trading profit for the year ended 31 March 2022. Use brackets for deductions and insert 0 (zero) if necessary, in order to fill in all unshaded boxes.

	£	£
Profit per accounts		656,980
	Add	Deduct
Depreciation charge		
Qualifying charitable donation		
Gifts to customers		
Accountancy and audit fee		
Legal fees – renewal of 20 year lease		
Legal fees – issue of debenture		
Repairs – knocked down wall		
Initial repairs to office		
Other expenses		
Debenture interest		
Bank interest		

	£	£
Dividends		
Capital allowances		
Interest payable on trading loans		
Net adjustments		
Taxable trading profit		

Task 7.2

Decide how each of the following items would be treated in the tax computation of a company with respect to its trading profits. Tick ONE box per line.

	Allow ✓	Disallow and add back ✓	Not taxable as trading income so deduct ✓
Dividends received from an unconnected company			
Profit on sale of shares			
Running costs of car with 20% private use by an employee			
Parking fine of director			
Capital allowances			
Director's salary			
Bank interest received			

Task 7.3

Righteous plc used to make its accounts up to 31 December. However, the directors decided to change the accounting date to 31 May and make up accounts for a 17-month period to 31 May 2022. The following information relates to the period of account from 1 January 2021 to 31 May 2022:

	£
Adjusted trading profit	500,000
Property business income	15,300
Capital gain on property sold on:	
1 May 2022	3,000
Qualifying charitable donations paid on:	
28 February 2021	15,000
31 August 2021	15,000
28 February 2022	40,000

No capital allowances are claimed.

Using the proforma layout provided, compute taxable total profits for the accounting periods based on the above accounts. Any amounts decreasing taxable profits should be shown as a negative figure (for example, a deduction of 5,000 should be shown as -5000 or -5,000). Leave boxes blank where no entry is required.

	First period £	Second period £
Trading profits		
Property business income		
Chargeable gain		
Qualifying charitable donations paid		
Taxable total profits	AUTOSUM	AUTOSUM

Task 7.4

When a company has a period of account which exceeds 12 months, how are the following apportioned:

	Time apportioned ✓	Period in which arises ✓	Separate computation ✓
Capital allowances			
Trading income			
Property income			
Investment income			
Chargeable gain			

Task 7.5

Rosemary Ltd has the following results for the ten-month period ended 31 March 2022:

	£
Taxable trading profits	600,000
Property business income	300,000
Dividends received	162,000

The corporation tax payable by Rosemary Ltd for period ended 31 March 2022 is:

£	

Task 7.6

In the year ended 31 March 2022, Thyme Ltd had taxable trading profits before capital allowances of £400,200. In February 2022 Thyme Ltd sold an asset for £200,000 resulting in a chargeable gain of £22,000. During the year Thyme Ltd accrued interest income of £12,000, earned property income of £8,000 and donated £6,000 to charity. Capital allowances for the year ended 31 March 2022 have been calculated as £24,000.

Calculate Thyme Ltd's corporation tax liability for the year ended 31 March 2022 by completing the table below. Any amounts decreasing taxable total profits should be shown with a negative figure (for example, a deduction of 5,000 should be shown as -5000 or -5,000). State all answers to the nearest pound.

	£
Trading profits after capital allowances	
Investment income	
Property income	
Chargeable gain	
Qualifying charitable donations	
Taxable total profit	AUTOSUM
Corporation tax liability	

Task 7.7

Identify whether the following statement is true or false.

A company usually pays corporation tax on dividend income.

	✓
True	
False	

Task 7.8

Identify which one of the following statements is true:

	✓
When a company has a long period of account, it prepares two tax computations for the period. The first one being for the first twelve months and the second being for the balance.	
When a company has a long period of account, the trading profits after capital allowances are prorated.	
When a company has a long period of account, the qualifying charitable donations are allocated to the period in which they accrue.	
A company can prepare a tax computation for a maximum period of 18 months.	

Task 7.9

Tarragon Ltd has the following results for the six-month period ended 31 March 2022:

	£
Taxable trading profits	200,000
Property income	50,000
Investment income	10,000
Dividends received	22,000
Dividends paid	30,000

The corporation tax payable by Tarragon Ltd for period ended 31 March 2022 is:

£	

QUESTIONS

Chapter 8 – Losses

Task 8.1

Pipchin has traded for many years, making up accounts to 30 September each year. His recent results have been:

Year ended	£
30 September 2019	12,000
30 September 2020	(45,000)
30 September 2021	8,000
30 September 2022	14,000

He has received property income as follows:

	£
2019/20	10,400
2020/21	11,000
2021/22	11,000
2022/23	11,000

Using the proforma layout provided, compute Pipchin's net income for 2019/20 to 2022/23, assuming maximum claims for loss relief are made as early as possible. If an answer is zero, insert 0, and show the offset of losses within brackets. Fill in all boxes.

	2019/20 £	2020/21 £	2021/22 £	2022/23 £
Trading profits				
Trading loss offset against future year				
Property income				
Trading loss offset against current year				
Trading loss offset against previous year				
Net income				

Task 8.2

Identify whether the following statement is true or false.

An individual can restrict a claim to set a trading loss against total income in order to have enough net income to use his personal allowance.

	✓
True	
False	

Task 8.3

Identify whether the following statement is true or false.

An individual must make a trading loss claim against total income in the tax year of the loss before making a claim to set the loss against total income in the preceding year.

	✓
True	
False	

Task 8.4

Identify whether the following statement is true or false.

An individual can only carry a trading loss forward against trading income of the same trade.

	✓
True	
False	

Task 8.5

Pennington Ltd produced the following results:

	Year ended 31 March		
	2020 £	2021 £	2022 £
Trading profit/(loss)	62,000	20,000	(83,000)
Investment income	1,200	600	1,200
Qualifying charitable donation	100	50	100

(a) **Using the proforma layout provided, compute Pennington Ltd's taxable total profits for the above accounting periods, assuming the loss relief is claimed as soon as possible. Fill in all boxes. Use brackets for loss relief and add a 0 (zero) where necessary.**

	Year ended 31 March		
	2020 £	2021 £	2022 £
Trading profits			
Investment income			
Total profits			
Current period loss relief			

	Year ended 31 March		
	2020 £	2021 £	2022 £
Carry back loss relief			
Total profits after loss relief			
Qualifying charitable donation			
Taxable total profits			

(b) **The trading loss available to carry forward at 31 March 2022 is:**

£	

Task 8.6

Ferraro Ltd has the following results.

	Year ended 30.6.19 £	9 months to 31.3.20 £	Year ended 31.3.21 £	Year ended 31.3.22 £
Trading profit (loss)	6,200	4,320	(100,000)	53,000
Bank deposit interest accrued	80	240	260	200
Rents receivable	1,420	1,440	1,600	1,500
Chargeable gain	–	12,680	–	–
Allowable capital loss	(5,000)	–	(9,423)	
Qualifying charitable donation	1,000	1,000	1,500	–

(a) **Using the proforma layout provided, compute all taxable total profits, claiming loss reliefs as early as possible. Fill in all boxes. Use brackets for loss relief and add a 0 (zero) where necessary.**

	Year ended 30.6.19 £	9 months to 31.3.20 £	Year ended 31.3.21 £	Year ended 31.3.22 £
Trading profits				
Investment income				
Property income				
Chargeable gains				
Total profits				

	Year ended 30.6.19 £	9 months to 31.3.20 £	Year ended 31.3.21 £	Year ended 31.3.22 £
Current period loss relief				
Carry back loss relief				
Carry forward loss relief				
Total profits after loss relief				
Qualifying charitable donation				
Taxable total profits				

(b) **The trading loss available to carry forward at 31 March 2022 is:**

£	

(c) **The capital loss available to carry forward at 31 March 2022 is:**

£	

Task 8.7

Identify whether the following statement is true or false.

A company must offset its trading loss against total profits in the loss-making period before carrying the loss back.

	✓
True	
False	

Task 8.8

Identify whether the following statement is true or false.

If a company carries a trading loss forward, the company can elect how much of the loss can be set against total profits in the following accounting period.

	✓
True	
False	

QUESTIONS

Task 8.9

Identify whether the following statement is true or false.

A company can set-off a capital loss against trading profits.

	✓
True	
False	

Task 8.10

Identify whether the following statements are true or false.

	True ✓	False ✓
When a company ceases trading, trading losses incurred in the 36 months prior to cessation can be carried back 12 months.		
Losses offset under terminal loss relief for companies are offset against the company's total profits (before QCDs)		
Losses offset under terminal loss relief are on a FIFO basis		
Losses offset under terminal loss relief for sole traders are offset against the individual's trading profits only		
Opening year loss relief is available to both companies and individuals		
Losses offset under opening year loss relief for sole traders are offset on a LIFO basis		
Losses offset under opening year loss relief for sole traders are offset against the individual's total income		

Task 8.11

Sally and Sara have run a profit-making partnership for many years, making profits which they shared equally. They prepare accounts to 5 April each year.

On 6 April 2021 Jo joined the partnership and the three partners agreed to share the profits equally. Sara left the partnership on 5 April 2022. Sally and Jo will share profits equally in future periods.

Taxable profits of the partnership are:

Year ended	Profits/(losses) £
5 April 2019	20,000
5 April 2020	40,000
5 April 2021	42,000
5 April 2022	(30,000)
5 April 2023 (projected)	20,000

Sally:

Sally has other property income of £15,000 per annum.

Sara:

Sara started a new job on 6 April 2022, earning a salary of £55,000. She has no other income.

Jo:

Until 5 April 2021, Jo was employed on an annual salary of £160,000. Jo has no other income

Explain the loss options available to EACH partner for the £10,000 loss they are each allocated for the tax year 2021/22, including a recommendation for the most appropriate option. You do not have to show detailed calculations but may use numbers to support your discussion.

Task 8.12

Osian makes a trading loss of £5,000 in 2021/22. He has property income of £6,300 in 2021/22. In 2020/21 Osian had taxable trading income of £15,000 and property income of £2,000.

(a) **Identify whether the following statements are true or false.**

	True ✓	False ✓
Osian can claim to use his loss of 2021/22 against his total income in 2020/21 only, in order to preserve his personal allowance in 2021/22.		
Osian can claim to use his loss of 2021/22 against his trading income in 2020/21 only, in order to preserve his personal allowance in 2021/22.		
Osian must claim to use his loss of 2021/22 against his total income in 2021/22, before being able to carry it back.		

(b) **Identify whether the following statements are true or false for a company.**

	True ✓	False ✓
When a trading loss is carried back by a company, it is set-off after deducting qualifying charitable donations.		
A company can carry a trade loss back 12 months against total profits and forward 36 months against profits of the same trade.		
A company must set-off trading losses in the current period before carrying back to the previous period.		

Chapter 9 – Self assessment for individuals

Task 9.1

Identify by which date an individual should normally submit their 2021/22 self-assessment tax return if it is to be filed online. Tick ONE box.

	✓
31 January 2023	
5 April 2023	
31 October 2022	
31 December 2022	

Task 9.2

Gordon had income tax payable of £14,500 in 2020/21. His income tax payable for 2021/22 was £20,500.

How will Gordon settle his income tax payable for 2021/22? Tick ONE box.

	✓
The full amount of £20,500 will be paid on 31 January 2023.	
Payments on account based on the estimated 2021/22 liability will be made on 31 January and 31 July 2022, with the balance payable on 31 January 2023.	
Payments on account of £10,250 will be made on 31 January and 31 July 2022 with nothing due on 31 January 2023.	
Payments on account of £7,250 will be made on 31 January and 31 July 2022, with the balance of £6,000 being paid on 31 January 2023.	

Task 9.3

The minimum penalty as a percentage of Potential Lost Revenue for a deliberate and concealed error on a tax return where there is a prompted disclosure is:

	✓
100%	
50%	
35%	
15%	

Task 9.4

Identify whether the following statement is true or false.

If an individual files her 2021/22 return online on 13 April 2023, the penalty for late filing is £100.

	✓
True	
False	

Task 9.5

Identify whether the following statement is true or false.

The penalty for failure to keep records is £3,000 per tax year or accounting period.

	✓
True	
False	

Task 9.6

Identify whether the following statement is true or false.

An individual is required to make a payment on account on 31 July 2022 for 2021/22. The payment is actually made on 10 November 2022.

The penalty payable is 5%.

	✓
True	
False	

Task 9.7

What is the latest date by which an individual must notify HMRC of chargeability to tax for 2021/22?

Enter the date in format (XX/XX/XXXX)

Task 9.8

Sylvia has been trading for many years. She filed her 2020/21 tax return, and paid the liability of £1,200, on 23 October 2022.

Calculate the penalty amounts that Sylvia will have to pay as a result of her late filing.

Penalty	£
Fixed penalty	
Daily penalty	
Tax-geared penalty	

State the latest date that HMRC can open an enquiry into Sylvia's 2020/21 tax return:

Enter the date in format (XX/XX/XXXX)

Task 9.9

Until what date should a sole trader keep their records supporting their 2021/22 tax return?

Enter the date in format (XX/XX/XXXX)

BPP LEARNING MEDIA

Chapter 10 – Self assessment for companies

Task 10.1

Boscobel plc has been a large company for corporation tax purposes for many years. For the year ending 31 March 2022, it had a corporation tax liability of £500,000.

Fill in the table below showing how it will pay its corporation tax liability.

Instalment	Due date (xx/xx/xxxx)	Amount due £
1		
2		
3		
4		

Task 10.2

Tick whether the following statements are true or false.

	True ✓	False ✓
A company with a period of account ending on 31 March 2022 must keep its records until 31 March 2024.		
An individual who becomes chargeable to income tax in 2021/22 must notify HMRC by 31 October 2022.		
A large company will not have to pay corporation tax by instalments if it has profits not exceeding £10m and was not large in the previous accounting period.		
A company which is not large (for corporation tax purposes) must pay its corporation tax by nine months and one day after the end of its accounting period.		

Task 10.3

A company receives a notice to file its return for the year ended 31 December 2021 on 28 November 2022.

The corporation tax return must be filed by:

A company receives a notice to file its return for the year ended 30 June 2021 on 15 July 2021.

The corporation tax return must be filed by:

Task 10.4

A company must keep its accounting records for [ ] years.

Failure to do so may incur a penalty of £ [ ] .

Task 10.5

Quasi Ltd filed its corporation tax return and paid the tax liability for the year ended 31 March 2022 on 31 July 2023. It showed a corporation tax liability of £10,000. What is the penalty payable for late filing of the return?

£ [ ]

Task 10.6

Vege Ltd filed its corporation tax return for the 18 months ending 31 July 2021 on 30 June 2022. By what date must HMRC give written notice of their intention to raise an enquiry into the return?

[ ]

Task 10.7

More Ltd prepares accounts to 30 September each year. It was given notice by HM Revenue & Customs (HMRC) to file its corporation tax return for the year to 30 September 2021 on 30 November 2021. The return was filed on 1 December 2022.

Calculate the penalty payable by More Ltd for the late filing of the return?

£ [ ]

Task 10.8

Little Fence Ltd has made up accounts for the 15-month period ended 31 March 2022.

By which date(s) must Little Fence Ltd file its corporation tax self-assessment tax return(s) for the 15-month period ended 31 March 2022?

- ○ The return for the year ended 31 December 2021 must be filed by 31 October 2022. The return for the period ended 31 March 2022 must be filed by 31 December 2022.
- ○ One return for the 15-month period ended 31 March 2022 must be filed by 31 March 2023.
- ○ The return for the year ended 31 December 2021 must be filed by 31 December 2022. The return for the period ended 31 March 2022 must be filed by 31 March 2023.
- ○ The returns for the year ended 31 December 2021 and the period ended 31 March 2022 must both be filed by 31 March 2023.

Task 10.9

Which of the following statements about penalties is true?

○ All businesses have penalties for late filing of returns, late payment of tax and late notification of chargeability.

○ Unincorporated businesses have penalties for late filing of returns, late payment of tax and late notification of chargeability whereas companies only have penalties for late filing and notification of chargeability.

○ Unincorporated businesses have penalties for late filing of returns and late payment of tax only whereas companies only have penalties for late filing.

○ All businesses have penalties for late filing of returns and late payment of tax only.

Chapter 11 – Chargeable gains for companies

Task 11.1

On 14 April 2021, Fire Ltd sold a factory for £230,000. This had originally been purchased in April 2003 for £160,000.

Assumed Indexation factor

April 2003 – December 2017 0.535

Using the proforma layout provided calculate the chargeable gain arising on the disposal of the factory. Fill in all boxes. Add a 0 (zero) if necessary.

	£
Proceeds	
Less cost	
Unindexed gain	
Less indexation allowance	
Chargeable gain/allowable loss	

Task 11.2

On 18 July 2021, Earth plc sold a warehouse for £180,000. This had been purchased in May 2006 for £100,000. Earth plc had spent £25,000 on an extension to the warehouse in August 2008.

Assumed Indexation factors

May 2006 – December 2017 0.407
May 2006 – August 2008 0.080
August 2008 – December 2017 0.280

Using the proforma layout provided calculate the chargeable gain arising on the disposal of the warehouse. Fill in all boxes. Add a 0 (zero) if necessary.

	£
Proceeds	
Less: cost	
enhancement expenditure	
Unindexed gain	
Less: indexation allowance on cost	
indexation allowance on enhancement	
Chargeable gain	

Task 11.3

Identify whether the following statement is true or false.

A company is entitled to an annual exempt amount.

	✓
True	
False	

Task 11.4

On 23 May 2018 Del Ltd sold a freehold property for £145,000 which had cost originally £50,000 on 9 May 2001. On 15 April 2021 Del Ltd acquired the freehold of another property for £140,000. Rollover relief was claimed.

Indexation factor

May 2001 – December 2017 0.560

(a) **The gain on disposal in May 2018 was:**

£	

(b) **The gain available for rollover relief is:**

£	

(c) **The base cost of the property acquired in April 2021 is:**

£	

Task 11.5

L plc sold a plot of land.

Tick the box that correctly finishes the following statement.

If L plc wishes to claim rollover relief it must acquire a new asset between:

	✓
The start of the previous accounting period and the end of the next accounting period	
Three years before and three years after the date of the disposal	
One year before and three years after the date of the disposal	
One year before and one year after the date of the disposal	

Task 11.6

Identify whether the following statements are true or false.

	True ✓	False ✓
If an asset is bought by a company prior to December 2017, indexation allowance will be available on disposal at a gain.		
Indexation on subsequent capital enhancement expenditure by a company must be calculated separately to the indexation on the original cost.		
No deduction is available for any legal fees associated with the sale of a chargeable asset.		
Indexation allowance can create a loss.		
Where only three quarters of a building is used for trading purposes, rollover relief is maximised by reinvesting the whole of the proceeds in a replacement asset.		
To qualify for rollover relief both the original asset and replacement asset must fall within the same category of qualifying asset.		
The reinvestment needs to take place in the three years before or 12 months after the disposal of the original asset.		

Task 11.7

On 10 January 2018 Edline Ltd acquired for £60,000 a small workshop where the company carried on a furniture making trade. On 6 August 2021 Edline Ltd sold the workshop for £125,000 having moved on 10 April 2021 to smaller premises which cost £123,500.

(a) **Edline Ltd's gain on the disposal before rollover relief is:**

£	

(b) **Assuming rollover relief is claimed, the gain immediately chargeable is:**

£	

(c) **The gain which Edline Ltd can rollover into the new premises is:**

£	

Chapter 12 – Share disposals

Task 12.1

Standring Ltd owned 20,000 shares in Smart plc acquired as follows:

5,000 shares acquired September 2001 for £10,000.
1 for 5 rights acquired October 2004 at £5 per share.
14,000 shares acquired August 2006 for £84,000.
Standring Ltd sold 18,000 shares in January 2022 for £155,000.

Indexation factors

September 2001 – October 2004	0.080
October 2004 – August 2006	0.056
August 2006 – December 2017	0.396

Using the proforma layout provided, calculate the chargeable gain arising on the sale in January 2022.

FA 1985 pool

	No. of shares	Original cost £	Indexed cost £

Gain

	£

Task 12.2

Box plc sold 11,000 shares in Crate Ltd for £78,200 on 25 May 2021. These shares had been acquired as follows.

26 May 1995	Purchased	4,000 shares for	£24,000
30 June 1996	1 for 2 bonus issue		
24 October 2003	Purchased	5,000 shares for	£27,500

Indexation factors

May 1995 – October 2003	0.221
May 1995 – June 1996	0.023
June 1996 – October 2003	0.193
October 2003 – December 2017	0.523

Using the proforma layout provided, calculate the gain on disposal.

FA 1985 pool

	No. of shares	Original cost £	Indexed cost £

Gain

	£

Task 12.3

Identify whether the following statement is true or false.

Indexation allowance on rights issue shares runs from the date of the rights issue even though the rights issue shares are treated as having been acquired at the time of the original acquisition to which they relate.

	✓
True	
False	

Task 12.4

Luna Ltd had the following transactions in shares during the year ended 31 March 2022:

(1) On 29 November 2021, Luna Ltd sold its entire shareholding of £1 ordinary shares in Pluto plc for £53,400. Luna Ltd had originally purchased these shares in Pluto plc on 14 June 2008 for £36,800.

(2) On 30 November 2021, Luna Ltd sold 10,000 of its shares in Neptune plc for £26,000. Luna Ltd had originally purchased 16,000 shares in Neptune plc on 10 May 2010 for £32,000.

Indexation factors are as follows:

June 2008–December 2017 = 0.283
May 2010–December 2017 = 0.244

What is Luna Ltd's chargeable gain on the sale of Pluto plc shares on 29 November 2021?

£	

What is the indexed cost of Luna Ltd's holding in Neptune Ltd immediately after the sale on 30 November 2021?

- ○ £12,000
- ○ £39,808
- ○ £24,880
- ○ £14,928

Task 12.5

Daisy Ltd had the following transactions in the shares of Dandelion Ltd:

5,000 shares purchased on 1 March 2012 at £4.20 per share.
1 for 2 bonus issue on 1 September 2014. The market value of the shares prior to the bonus issue was £6.00 per share.
4,000 shares purchased on 15 August 2018 for £7.50 per share.
1,000 shares purchased on 8 September 2021 for £8.00 per share.
2,000 shares sold on 11 September 2021 for £8.60 per share.

Indexation factors

March 2012 – September 2014	0.070
September 2014 – December 2017	0.080
March 2012 – December 2017	0.155

(a) Complete the share pool for Daisy Ltd. The purchase on 1 March 2012 has already been included. Show the balance of the shares carried forward. Show your answers to the nearest pound. You have been given more space than you will need.

	Number of shares	Cost £	Indexed cost £
1 March 2012 - purchase	5,000	21,000	21,000

(a) Calculate the chargeable gain or allowable loss on the disposal of the shares in Dandelion Ltd by Daisy Ltd on 11 September 2021. Show your answer to the nearest pound.

	£

Chapter 13 – Business Disposals

Task 13.1

Romana purchased a factory for £40,000. She then spent £5,000 building a new extension on the factory. She sold the factory for £90,600 on 15 March 2022. Romana had not made any other disposals during 2021/22.

What is her taxable gain for 2021/22?

	✓
£33,300	
£38,300	
£45,600	
£50,600	

Task 13.2

Jack sells an asset in December 2021 and makes a chargeable gain of £15,000. Jack is an additional rate taxpayer.

At what rate would Jack pay capital gains tax on this gain?

Task 13.3

Gayle made chargeable gains of £3,000 in August 2021 and £18,100 in November 2021. She has unused basic rate band of £5,000 in 2021/22.

Gayle's capital gains tax liability for 2021/22 is:

£	

Task 13.4

Gerry made chargeable gains of £27,100 in December 2021. She made no other disposals in the year. Her taxable income (ie after deducting the personal allowance) for 2021/22 was £26,205. Note the limit for the basic rate band for 2021/22 is £37,700.

Gerry's capital gains tax liability for 2021/22 is:

£	

Task 13.5

Ronald started in business as a sole trader in August 2007. He acquired a freehold shop for £80,000 and a warehouse for £150,000.

He sold his business as a going concern to Lesley in December 2021 and received £50,000 for goodwill, £90,000 for the shop and £130,000 for the warehouse. Ronald made no other chargeable gains in 2021/22 and he is a higher rate taxpayer.

Using the proforma layout provided, compute the CGT payable by Ronald for 2021/22. Fill in all unshaded boxes. Use a 0 (zero) if necessary.

	£	£
Proceeds of goodwill		
Less cost		
Gain/(loss) on goodwill		
Proceeds of shop		
Less cost		
Gain/(loss) on shop		
Proceeds of warehouse		
Less cost		
Gain/(loss) on warehouse		
Net gains eligible for business asset disposal relief		
Less annual exempt amount		
Taxable gains		
CGT payable		

Task 13.6

Identify whether the following statement is true or false.

The lifetime limit of gains eligible for business asset disposal relief is £1,000,000.

	✓
True	
False	

Task 13.7

Simon acquired 10,000 Blue Ltd shares worth £65,000 in September 1992 as a gift from his father. His father had originally acquired them as an investment in 1987 and gift relief was claimed on the gain of £15,000. Simon sold the Blue Ltd shares for £200,000 on 30 November 2021. He has no other assets for CGT purposes and made no other disposals in 2021/22.

The taxable gain arising on the sale of the Blue Ltd shares is:

£	

Task 13.8

Fran gave a factory worth £500,000 to her friend Anna on 1 June 2021 and a claim for gift relief was made. Fran had bought the factory on 1 January 2009 for £75,000. On 1 July 2022 Anna sold the factory for £520,000.

(a) **Fran's chargeable gain on her disposal is:**

£	

(b) **Anna's chargeable gain (before deduction of the annual exempt amount) on her disposal is:**

£	

Task 13.9

State whether the following statements are true or false by ticking in the appropriate box

	True ✓	False ✓
Business asset disposal relief will be available on the disposal of a 6% shareholding in L Ltd, an unquoted trading company which has been held for three years. The shareholder has worked for the company for five years.		
Business asset disposal relief will be available on the disposal of a 6% shareholding in L Ltd, an unquoted investment company which has been held for three years. The shareholder has worked for the company for five years.		
Gains of £2 million on disposal of a business owned for five years are taxed at 10%.		

Task 13.10

David is retiring and plan to sell his business on 1 January 2022. His assets at the date of sale are detailed below.

Identify the impact that the sale of each of the assets described below will have for tax purposes by dragging the appropriate response into the 'Impact' column. Each response can be used more than once.

Asset	Market value £	Original cost £	TWDV £	Impact
Factory	95,000	110,000		
Warehouse	95,000	80,000		
Plant & machinery	1,000	10,000	5,000	
Goodwill	32,000	0		
Inventory	8,000	6,000		

Drag and drop options:

Chargeable gain
Capital loss
Increase trading profit
Decrease trading profit

Task 13.11

Anna is an additional rate tax payer for income tax purposes. On 31 December 2021 she sold her sole trade business which she set up in 2010. She sold her business for £536,000 with her assets as stated below:

Asset	Market value £	Original cost £	TWDV £
Factory	300,000	220,000	
Warehouse	100,000	105,000	
Plant & machinery	5,000	22,000	10,000
Goodwill	96,000	0	
Inventory	35,000	32,000	

The income tax and national insurance contributions saved from the adjustments due to Anna selling the plant and machinery and inventory is £940. Anna's annual exempt amount has already been used against non-business gains.

(a) **Calculate the taxable gain for Anna on disposal of her business.**

£	

(b) **Calculate the tax that will be charged on the gain assuming that Anna claims all beneficial reliefs.**

£	

(c) **Calculate the after-tax proceeds that Anna will have made from the sale of her business.**

£	

Task 13.12

Paul sold his shares in Oak Ltd on 1 January 2022 for £420,000. He is the sole shareholder and director of Oak Ltd, an unquoted trading company, and had bought his shares for £20,000 in 2000. Paul has no other disposals during 2021/22, is a higher rate tax payer and has already had £900,000 of taxable gains on which business asset disposal relief has been claimed.

Calculate Paul's taxable gain from the sale of his shares.

£	

Calculate the tax that will be charged on Paul's taxable gains assuming all beneficial claims are made.

£	

Calculate Paul's after-tax proceeds from the sale of his shares.

£	

Chapter 14 - Tax Planning for Businesses

Task 14.1

When deciding whether a trade is being carried on, HM Revenue and Customs is often guided by the badges of trade.

Write a memo to a client who is concerned they may be trading, explain the badges of trade that are used to indicate whether a trade is being carried on.

From:	AAT student
To:	A Client
Date:	Today
Subject:	Badges of trade

This page is for the continuation of your memo. You may not need all of it.

Task 14.2

Peter has a hobby restoring antique books. He has just sold a restored book that he has owned for several years. He sold 12 restored books in 2021/22.

Identify which TWO of the following badges indicate that Peter is carrying on a trade in relation to his disposal:

	Trade ✓
The number of transactions	
Interval of time between purchase and sale	
Changes to the asset	
Correction of own work	

Task 14.3

Sarah is currently self-employed. She extracts £40,000 each year as drawings.

She also has a part time job earning employment income of £12,570 and receives dividends of £2,000 each year from investments she has.

Sarah is considering changing so that her business is run through a company from 6 April 2021. The forecast taxable total profits of the new limited company for the year ended 5 April 2022 will be £50,000 (before taking account of any director's remuneration). Sarah will pay herself gross director's remuneration of £30,000 and dividends of £10,000. The balance of the profits will remain undrawn within the new company. She will be the sole director and shareholder of the company.

(a) **Explain how the expected profits of the year ended 5 April 2022 will be taxed dependent on whether Sarah continues as a sole trader or changes to operating through a company. You are not required to complete tax computations.**

(b) Advise Sarah as to why her proposed basis of extracting profits from the new company is not optimum for tax purposes, and explain how Sarah's mix of director's remuneration and dividends could be improved to reduce her own total tax liability. You are not required to complete tax computations.

Task 14.4

Identify whether the following statements are true or false.

	True ✓	False ✓
Employer's NIC is due at 13.8% on any salary paid in excess of £9,568.		
Dividends paid are not tax deductible for the company.		
An additional rate tax payer will pay income tax at 32.5% on any dividend income received.		
Any salary and employee's NICs thereon are tax deductible for the company.		
A company with a single director and no other employees is not entitled to the £4,000 employment allowance.		

Task 14.5

Identify whether the following statements are true or false.

	True ✓	False ✓
A sole trader is a separate legal entity		
Incorporated businesses must follow more rules and regulations		
The employment allowance is available to a partnership.		
A sole trader pays income tax and employee's NIC on their profits.		
Companies can take a corporation tax deduction for any salary and employer's NIC.		

Task 14.6

Matilda is the sole director and shareholder of a small company, Tilly Ltd. Tilly Ltd has no employees. Tilly Ltd's profits (for both tax and accounting purposes) are expected to be £200,000 before corporation tax each year.

In addition to her work for Tilly Ltd, Matilda also has other income from employment of £180,000 and dividend income of £10,000 making her an additional rate taxpayer.

If Matilda chose to extract her profits by way of the maximum possible dividend , calculate the maximum dividends that she will receive?

£	

How much after-tax cash would Matilda receive if she extracted the maximum possible dividend?

£	

If Matilda chose to extract her profits by way of the maximum salary, what salary would she receive?

£	

How much post-tax cash would Matilda receive if she extracted the maximum possible salary?

£	

Task 14.7

Anne and Vlad are a married couple. Anne works full time earning a salary of £160,000 and Vlad works part time earning a salary £10,000. The couple are considering setting up in partnership.

Identify which profit share would minimise the couple's overall income tax liability.

(a) 50% Anne, 50% Vlad

(b) 80% Anne, 20% Vlad

(c) 20% Anne, 80% Vlad

Task 14.8

Complete the following sentence by filling in the gap.

When an asset is passed between a married couple/ civil partners the asset transfers at

[▼] for capital gains tax purposes.

Picklist:

Nil gain/ nil loss
Market value
Nil proceeds

Answer Bank

Chapter 1 – Tax framework

Task 1.1

	Incorporated ✓	Unincorporated ✓
Sole trader		✓
Partnership		✓
Limited company	✓	

Task 1.2

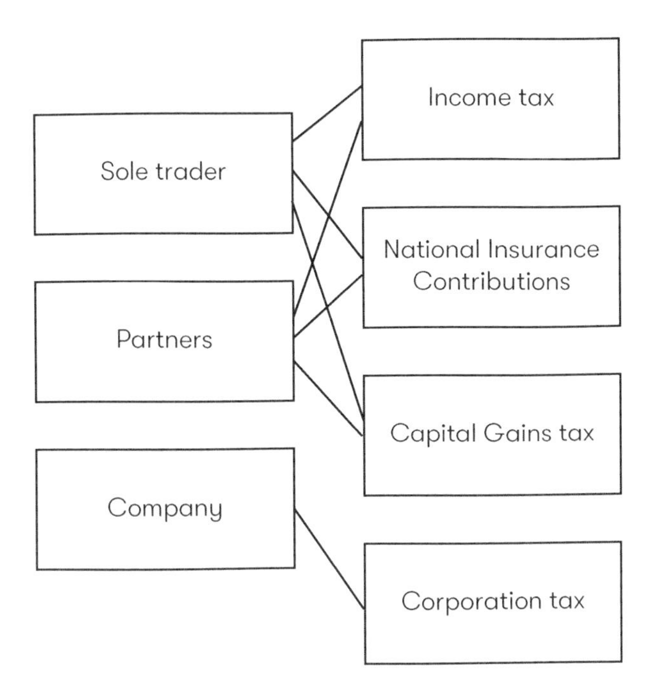

Task 1.3

	Force of law ✓	No force of law ✓
Statute law	✓	
Act of Parliament	✓	
Statutory Instrument	✓	
HMRC guidance		✓
Case Law	✓	

ANSWERS

Task 1.4

	✓
Claiming capital allowances on a fictitious piece of equipment	
Failing to notify HMRC of a profitable trade commenced three years ago	
Obtaining tax-free interest by investing in an ISA	✓
Deciding not to declare rental income received	

Task 1.5

Ethical duties and responsibilities of an AAT accountant (Any two of the following):

Maintain client confidentiality at all times

Adopt an ethical approach and maintain an objective outlook

Give timely and constructive advice to clients

Honest and professional conduct with HMRC

Task 1.6

Tax [avoidance] is the use of loopholes in tax legislation to minimise tax liabilities.

Tax [planning] is the use of all available reliefs in the manner intended to minimise tax liabilities.

Tax [evasion] is the deliberate misleading of tax authorities to minimise tax liabilities.

Task 1.7

	✓
7.5%	
20%	
32.5%	
40%	✓

Jamie is a higher rate taxpayer due to the level of his employment income. Therefore his savings income (bank interest) will be taxed at the higher rate for savings income (40%).

Task 1.8

	✓
Consider making a money laundering report	✓
Tell the client that you are making a money laundering report	
Cease to act for the client	✓
Advise HMRC of the omission	

You should cease to act for the client and tell HMRC that you have ceased acting (without telling them why). You should consider making a money laundering report. You should not advise HMRC of the omission as this would breach your duty of confidentiality. You should not tell the client that you are making a money laundering report as this would constitute the offence of tipping off.

Task 1.9

	Tax evasion ✓	Tax planning ✓
Gifting an asset to a spouse in order to reduce a capital gains tax liability		✓
Omitting an invoice from accounting records to push it into the following tax year	✓	
Offering customers a discount for paying cash but not including these cash payments in the accounts or tax return	✓	
Passing shares between spouses so that the dividend income is taxed on the spouse paying the lower rate of income tax		✓
Delaying the sale of an asset so that the disposal falls into the next tax year so as to utilise next year's annual exempt amount		✓

Task 1.10

- Enid should be advised to disclose details of the profits to HMRC
- If Enid does not disclose the profits to HMRC, your firm would be obliged to report under the money laundering regulations

Your firm should also consider ceasing to act for Enid. If it does cease to act, your firm should notify HMRC that it no longer acts for her although your firm should not provide any reason for this.

Task 1.11

Tax evasion is illegal	TRUE	
Both tax evasion and tax avoidance are illegal		FALSE
Tax avoidance is legal but may fail if challenged in the courts by HMRC	TRUE	
Tax evasion always involves providing HMRC with false information		FALSE

Tax evasion does not necessarily involve providing HMRC with false information. It could also include failing to disclose information.

Task 1.12

- Reporting under the money laundering regulations
- Advising the client to make disclosure

Your firm should advise the client to make disclosure and your firm should make a report under the money laundering regulations.

You should not inform HMRC of the non-disclosure. Your firm also should not warn the client that it will be reporting the non-disclosure as this might constitute the criminal offence of 'tipping-off'.

Task 1.13

The three fundamental principles threatened by this situation are integrity, objectivity and professional behaviour.

Task 1.14

(a) Spruce Ltd

Actions to take:

- Check client files to establish the correct repayment due.
- Contact client to explain if this is an HMRC error and tell them not to spend the money.
- Check the engagement letter to see if there is authority to advice HMRC of the error, and if there is then inform HMRC of the error
- If there is no authority, ask the client for authority to inform HMRC/ ask Spanner Ltd to inform HMRC
- Warn Spanner Ltd of consequences of them not disclosing the error- interest, penalties and criminal prosecution
- If Spanner Ltd refuses to notify HMRC of the error, cease to act for them
- All actions need to be documented.

(b) **Jack**

The three fundamental principles threatened are:

- Confidentiality
- Objectivity
- Professional behaviour

Task 1.15

(a) Tax planning is the legal method of reducing your tax liability and does not involve misleading HMRC.

Tax evasion is the deliberate suppression of information such as deliberately not telling them about the new business. Tax evasion could also be via deliberately providing false information.

Tax evasion is a criminal offence punishable by fines and/or imprisonment.

(b) The fundamental principles threatened include objectivity, if the promise of work influences judgement.

There is a threat to integrity which would be breached by submitting false information to HMRC.

There is a threat to professional behaviour as this requires complying with the tax laws. If a business fails

Task 1.16

	Tax evasion	Not tax evasion
Deciding not to declare trading income earned	✓	
Failing to notify HMRC of starting to earn rental income	✓	
Claiming capital allowances on a non-existent piece of plant or machinery	✓	

Earning tax free dividends in an ISA is a legitimate way to reduce tax.

Chapter 2 – Computing trading income

Task 2.1

£5,400

Depreciation and customer entertaining are not deductible and must be added back. The amount added back is therefore £(3,000 + 2,400) = £5,400.

Staff entertaining is fully deductible (the £150 limit applies to the taxable benefit for the employees).

Task 2.2

	Allow ✓	Disallow and add back ✓	Not taxable so deduct ✓
Gifts of 30 bottles of wine to clients		✓	
Lease costs of a car with emissions of 60g/km		✓ (15%)	
Costs of £5,000 to repair a roof	✓		
£1,000 cost to register a patent	✓		
Accounting profit on disposal of a van			✓
£500 donation to a political party		✓	
Depreciation		✓	

Task 2.3

	£	£
Profit for the year per accounts		5,300
	Add	Deduct
Staff wages	0	0
Mr Jelly's salary (N1)	260	0
Light and heat	0	0
Motor expenses (N2) (£350 × 1/7)	50	0
Postage, stationery and telephone	0	0
Painting shop internally	0	0
Plant repairs	0	0
Stockroom extension (N3)	101	0
Provision (N4)	200	0
Donations (N2)	10	0
Advertising	0	0

	£	£
Entertaining (N5)	90	0
Gifts (N6)	70	0
Legal expenses	0	0
Depreciation charge	600	0
Total net adjustments		1,381
Taxable trading profit		6,681

Notes.

1 Appropriation of profit
2 Not expenditure incurred wholly and exclusively for the purpose of trade
3 Capital items
4 Increase in general provision is disallowed
5 Entertaining expenses specifically disallowed
6 Gifts of alcohol specifically disallowed

Task 2.4

	Allow ✓	Disallow and add back ✓	Not taxable so deduct ✓
Increase in specific provision	✓		
Decrease in general provision			✓
Depreciation charge		✓	
Cocktail party held for customers		✓	
Political donation		✓	
Employees salary	✓		
Repair to factory roof	✓		

Task 2.5

Bill	Taxable trading income	Election required? (Y/N)
Expenses of £200	Nil	N
Expenses of £900	(100)	Y

With receipts not exceeding £1,000 Bill's trading assessment will be nil due to the trading allowance.

However, with expenses of £900 Bill is better off electing to disapply the trading allowance and instead choosing to calculate his trading assessment in the normal way as income minus expenses. This way he will be able to use the loss to save tax.

Belinda	Taxable trading income	Election required? (Y/N)
Expenses of £1,200	300	N
Expenses of £300	500	Y

With receipts exceeding £1,000 Belinda's trading assessment will automatically be calculated in the normal way as income minus expenses.

However, with expenses of only £300 Belinda is better off electing to deduct the trading allowance instead of expenses ie £1,500 – £1,000.

Task 2.6

	£
Accounting profit	22,000
Depreciation	900
Donation	800
Repairs	0
Legal fees	700
Goods taken for own use	600
Capital allowances	-500
Taxable profit	24,500

Task 2.7

	£
Accounting profit	46,000
Depreciation	3,600
Bad debt	0
Parking fines	0
Client entertaining	800
Local charity	0
Capital allowances	-1,000
Taxable profit	49,400

Task 2.8

	Deductible/ Revenue ✓	Disallowable/ Capital ✓
Decorating office premises	✓	
Repairs to a tractor to make it usable		✓
Replacing single glazed windows with double glazed equivalents	✓	
Legal fees on renewal of a 48 year lease	✓	
Legal fees on purchase of a 30 year lease		✓
Legal fees on renewal of a 60 year lease		✓

Task 2.9

	No adjustment ✓	Add back ✓	Deduct ✓
Purchase of raw materials	✓		
Private use of vehicle by an employee	✓		
Loan to former employee written off		✓	
Interest received on business bank account			✓

Task 2.10

Profit	172,820
Items added back	
Qualifying charitable donation	5,000
Parking fines paid for a director	160
Depreciation	65,230
Donation to a political party	850
Total added back	71,240
Items deducted	
Profit on sale of shares	45,777
Dividends received	40,500
Capital allowances	38,750
Total deducted	125,027
Adjusted trading profits	119,033

Chapter 3 – Capital allowances

Task 3.1

	Revenue ✓	Capital ✓	Capital allowances - P&M	Capital allowances - SBAs
Purchase of machinery		✓	✓	
Rent paid for premises	✓			
Insurance of premises	✓			
Repairs to roof of factory	✓			
New extension to shop		✓		✓
Installation of new picture window		✓		
Purchase of new car for owner		✓	✓	
Legal fees relating to purchase of new factory		✓		
Payment of staff wages	✓			
Accountancy costs	✓			
Redecoration of shop	✓			
Construction of a warehouse		✓		✓

Task 3.2

	AIA	General pool	Private use asset Mercedes car (80%)	Total allowances
p/e 28 February 2022				
b/f		38,500		
Additions				
14.1.21 Factory machinery	1,633,333			
30.3.21 Car			18,000	
31.3.21 Car		8,000		
2.6.21 Equipment	31,000			
Disposals				
31.12.21 Machinery		(3,000)		
AIA (note)	(1,500,000)			1,500,000
Transfer to main pool	(164,333)	164,333		
		207,833		

	AIA	General pool	Private use asset Mercedes car (80%)	Total allowances
WDA @ 18% × 18/12		(56,115)		56,115
WDA @ 18% × 18/12			(4,860) × 80%	3,888
c/f		151,718	13,140	
Allowances				1,560,003

Note. Maximum AIA = (£1,000,000 × 18/12) = £1,500,000

Task 3.3

	AIA	FYA	General pool	Total allowances
Y/e 31 March 2022				
Additions				
6.5.21 Machinery	1,050,000			
6.7.21 Low emission car		8,000		
31.8.21 Car			10,500	
AIA (max)	(1,000,000)			1,000,000
	50,000			
Transfer to main pool	(50,000)		50,000	
			60,500	
FYA @ 100%		(8,000)		8,000
		–		
WDA @ 18%			(10,890)	10,890
c/f			49,610	
Total allowances				1,018,890

Task 3.4

	General pool	Private use asset 1 Car (1) @ 70%	Special rate pool	Private use asset 2 Car (2) @ 70%	Total allowances
P/e 30 September 2021					
TWDV b/f	120,000	21,000	17,500		
Addition					
10.8.21 Car				25,000	
Disposal					
10.8.21 Car		(16,000)			
Balancing allowance		5,000 × 70%			3,500

	General pool	Private use asset 1 Car (1) @ 70%	Special rate pool	Private use asset 2 Car (2) @ 70%	Total allowances
WDA @ 18% × $\frac{6}{12}$	(10,800)				10,800
WDA @ 6% × $\frac{6}{12}$			(525)		525
WDA @ 6% × $\frac{6}{12}$				(750) × 70%	525
TWDV c/f	109,200		16,975	24,250	
Allowances					15,350

Task 3.5

	AIA	FYA	Super deduction	General pool	Special rate pool	Private use asset	Total allowances
Y/e 28 February 2022							
TWDV b/f				106,000			
Addition - car					14,000		
Addition - machinery			32,000				
Super deduction (×1.3)			(32,000)				41,600
Disposal - car				(3,000)			
				103,000			
WDA @ 18%				(18,540)			18,540
WDA @ 6%					(840)		840
TWDV c/f				84,460	13,160		
Allowances							60,980

Note. That we only ever restrict allowances for assets with private use by the proprietor (ie. sole trader or partner, NOT employees) therefore there will never be private use adjustments in a company's capital allowances workings.

ANSWERS

Task 3.6

Davies Ltd – Capital allowances for year ended 31 March 2022

	FYA	AIA	Super deduction	General pool	Special rate pool	Allowances
TWDV b/f				180,000		
Machine		1,260,000				
AIA (Max)		(1,000,000)				1,000,000
		260,000				
To pool		(260,000)		260,000		
Computer			12,000			
Super-deduction (×1.3)			(12,000)			15,600
Car					22,000	
Disposal				(12,000)		
				428,000	22,000	
WDA × 18%				(77,040)		77,040
WDA × 6%					(1,320)	1,320
TWDV c/f				350,960	20,680	1,093,960

Note. the 130% super deduction is not available on second hand assets, nor on cars, so in this question is only available on the computer.

Task 3.7

	AIA	FYA	Super deduction	General Pool	Special rate pool	Private use asset	Allowances
TWDV b/f				230,000			
Additions qualifying for super deduction							
Machinery			75,000				
Super deduction (note)			(75,000)				97,500
Additions not qualifying for the AIA or super deduction							
BMW (Car)				19,000			
Audi (Car)					25,000		
Disposal							
Machine				(6,600)			

	AIA	FYA	Super deduction	General Pool	Special rate pool	Private use asset	Allowances
				242,400			
WDA × 18% × 9/12				(32,724)			32,724
WDA × 6% × 9/12					(1,125)		1,125
				209,676	23,875		131,349

Note. The super deduction is available for the machine purchase, and is more beneficial than the AIA. The super-deduction is not pro-rated for a short accounting period.

Task 3.8

Jav

Accounting period	SBA
y/e 31 March 2022	£2,250
y/e 31 March 2023	£13,500
y/e 31 March 2024	£13,500
y/e 31 March 2025	£6,750

Sarah

Accounting period	SBA
y/e 31 December 2024	£3,375
y/e 31 December 2025	£13,500

Working

Jav

y/e 31 March 2022: £450,000 x 3% x 2/12 = £2,250

y/e 31 March 2023: £450,000 x 3% = £13,500

y/e 31 March 2024: £450,000 x 3% = £13,500

y/e 31 March 2025: £450,000 x 3% x 6/12 = £6,750

Sarah

y/e 31 December 2024: £450,000 x 3% x 3/12 = £3,375

y/e 31 December 2025: £450,000 x 3% = £13,500

The SBA is based on Jav's qualifying expenditure of £450,000. Jav can claim the SBA from the date that the factory is brought into use. Sarah's SBAs are calculated on the original qualifying expenditure of £450,000 (not her acquisition cost). The SBAs are pro-rated in the accounting periods of acquisition and disposal.

Task 3.9

	SBA ✓
Purchase of a factory in Nottingham from a sole trader for £800,000. The factory was constructed in 2000.	
Purchase of a newly constructed storage warehouse from a developer for £3m	✓
Purchase of a brownfield site for £1m to build a new factory on	
Stamp Duty Land Tax on the cost of a newly built factory	
Construction costs of a new office block	✓

SBAs are only available on new commercial structures and buildings constructed (or renovated) from October 2018.

SBAs are not available on the cost of the land or stamp taxes.

Task 3.10

Year ended 31 March 2022

	FYA	AIA	General pool	Private use asset 1	Private use asset 2	Total allowances
b/f			13,291	8,745		
AIA additions						
April 2021		258,100				
June 2021		983,750				
Car April 2021	24,500					
AIA (max)		(1,000,000)				1,000,000
Transfer to pool		(241,850)	241,850			
Disposals			(4,100)	(8,000)		
			251,041			
BA				745 × 70%		522
WDA @ 18%			(45,187)			45,187
FYA @ 100%	(24,500)				× 60%	14,700
c/f			205,854	0	0	
Total allowances						1,060,409

Note. Full credit would also have been awarded if Mustafa's car had been entered into the Private Use asset 2 column provided that it was clear that the car was eligible for a 100% FYA. As this Task is human marked there is some flexibility for alternative presentations.

Chapter 4 – Taxing unincorporated businesses

Task 4.1

Her first tax year is:

2019/20

Her taxable profits in her first tax year of trading are:

£	6,188

Her taxable profits in her second tax year of trading are:

£	24,750

Her taxable profits in her third tax year of trading are:

£	24,750

Overlap profits are:

£	22,688

Working

Taxable profits

Tax year	Basis period	Taxable profits £
2019/20	(1.1.20 – 5.4.20) £33,000 × $^{3}/_{16}$ =	6,188
2020/21	(6.4.20 – 5.4.21) £33,000 × $^{12}/_{16}$ =	24,750
2021/22	(1.5.20 – 30.4.21) £33,000 × $^{12}/_{16}$ =	24,750

Overlap profits

The profits taxed twice are those for the period 1 May 2020 to 5 April 2021: $^{11}/_{16}$ × £33,000

Task 4.2

Mr Phone's basis period for 2019/20 runs from:

01/07/2019

to:

05/04/2020

Mr Phone's basis period for 2020/21 runs from:

01/07/2019

to:

30/06/2020

His taxable profits in his second tax year of trading are:

£	23,500

Overlap profits are:

£	19,500

Working

Tax year	Basis period	Taxable profits £
2019/20	Actual	
	1 July 2019 to 5 April 2020	
	(9/11 × £22,000)	18,000
2020/21	First 12 months	
	1 July 2019 to 30 June 2020	
	£22,000 + (1/12 × £18,000)	23,500
2021/22	(CYB)	
	Year ended 31 May 2021	18,000

	£
Overlap period is 1 July 2019 to 5 April 2020	18,000
and 1 June 2020 to 30 June 2020	
(1/12 × £18,000)	1,500
	19,500

Task 4.3

Mr Mug's final tax year is:

2021/22

Mr Mug's penultimate tax year is:

2020/21

His taxable profits in his final tax year of trading are:

£	11,000

Working

		£
2021/22	1 May 2020 to 31 December 2021 (16,000 + 4,000)	20,000
	Less overlap relief	(9,000)
		11,000

Note. Year ended 30 April 2020 was assessed in 2020/21.

Task 4.4

Jackie's first tax year is:

2017/18

Her taxable profits in her first tax year of trading are:

£	13,200

Jackie's second tax year is:

2018/19

Her taxable profits in her second tax year of trading are:

£	14,400

Jackie's final tax year is:

2021/22

Her taxable profits in her final tax year of trading are:

£	300

Over the life of her business Jackie is assessed on total profits of:

£	48,240

Working

Tax year	Basis period	Taxable profits £
2017/18	First year – 1.5.17 to 5.4.18	
	11/15 × £18,000	13,200
2018/19	Second year 12 months to 31.7.18 (1.8.17 – 31.7.18)	
	12/15 × £18,000	14,400
2019/20	Third year y/e 31.7.19	11,700
2020/21	y/e 31.7.20	8,640
2021/22	Y/e 31.7.21	4,800
	P/e 28.2.22	5,100
		9,900
	Less overlap profits	(9,600)
		300

Overlap profits

Overlap period is 1 August 2017 to 5 April 2018, ie 8/15 × £18,000 = £9,600

ANSWERS

Task 4.5

	31 March ✓	30 April ✓
Harry is just starting his business and is expecting large profits initially. He would like to avoid overlap profits.	✓	
Javier is having some cash flow problems and would like the maximum possible time to pay his tax.		✓

Task 4.6

Start date	6 April 2021

End date	5 April 2022

2021/22 is the second year of trading. There is no accounting date ending in this year so the actual basis applies.

Task 4.7

First tax year (2019/20): Actual basis 1.2.20 to 5.4.20

Second tax year (2020/21): First 12 months of trading 1.2.20 to 31.1.21

Third tax year (2021/22): Current year basis 1.12.20 to 30.11.21

Periods of overlap:

		£
1.2.20 to 5.4.20	2/10 × £30,000	6,000
1.12.20 to 31.1.21	2/12 × £42,000	7,000
		13,000

Task 4.8

Final tax year: 2021/22	£
y/e 31.12.21	18,000
p/e 31.3.22	3,000
Less overlap profits	(2,000)
	19,000

Chapter 5 – Partnerships

Task 5.1

	Total £	Fimbo £	Florrie £	Pom £
12 months to 31 December 2020				
Salary	5,000	5,000	0	0
Share of profits	5,000	3,000	2,000	0
Total for year	10,000	8,000	2,000	0
12 months to 31 December 2021				
Salary	5,000	5,000	0	0
Share of profits	15,000	9,000	6,000	0
Total for year	20,000	14,000	6,000	0
12 months to 31 December 2022				
Salary	6,500	6,500	0	0
Share of profits	18,500	6,167	6,167	6,166
Total for year	25,000	12,667	6,167	6,166

Task 5.2

(a)

	Total £	John £	Paul £	George £
Period ended 31 July 2019				
Division of profits	24,300	9,720	7,290	7,290
Year ended 31 July 2020				
Division of profits	16,200	6,480	4,860	4,860
Year ended 31 July 2021				
Division of profits	14,900	5,960	4,470	4,470

(b)

	John £	Paul £	George £
2018/19	4,166	3,124	3,124
2019/20	12,420	9,315	9,315
2020/21	6,480	4,860	4,860
2021/22	5,960	4,470	4,470

Working

	John £	Paul £	George £
2018/19			
1 January 2019 – 5 April 2019			
3/7 × £(9,720/7,290/7,290)	4,166	3,124	3,124
2019/20			
(1 January 2019 to 31 December 2019)			
1 January 2019 to 31 July 2019	9,720	7,290	7,290
1 August 2019 to 31 December 2019			
5/12 × £(6,480/4,860/4,860)	2,700	2,025	2,025
	12,420	9,315	9,315
2020/21			
Year ended 31 July 2020	6,480	4,860	4,860
2021/22			

Task 5.3

Year ended 31 December 2021	Total £	Strange £	Pavin £	Lehman £
To 31 July 2021				
Salaries (15,000/5000 × 7/12)	11,667	8,750	2,917	0
Interest on capital (20,000/10,000 × 5% × 7/12)	875	583	292	0
Division of profits (48,000 × 7/12 – 11,667 – 875)	15,458	7,729	5,153	2,576
To 31 December 2021				
Salary (20,000 × 5/12)	8,333	8,333	0	0
Division of profits (48,000 × 5/12 – 8,333)	11,667	4,667	4,667	2,333
Total for year ended 31 December 2021	48,000	30,062	13,029	4,909

Task 5.4

Year ended 31 May 2021	Total £	Bob £	Annie £	John £
To 31 January 2021				
Salaries	30,000	10,000	10,000	10,000
Division of profits	30,000	15,000	7,500	7,500
To 31 May 2021				
Salaries	10,000	0	5,000	5,000
Division of profits	20,000	0	10,000	10,000
Total for year ended 31 May 2021	90,000	25,000	32,500	32,500

Task 5.5

£44,150

	£
1.8.20 to 31.8.20 1/12 × £96,000 × 1/2	4,000
1.9.20 to 31.7.21 Salary 11/12 × £9,000	8,250
1.9.20 to 31.7.21 Profit share ((11/12 × £96,000) – 8,250) × 2/5	31,900
	44,150

Task 5.6

Robin and Stuart each	£48,000

Tania	£5,600

Robin and Stuart

CYB y/e 31.12.21 £96,000 × 1/2 = £48,000

Tania

Actual basis 1.1.22 – 5.4.22 £112,000 × 1/5 × 3/12 = £5,600

ANSWERS

Chapter 6 – National insurance

Task 6.1

The Class 2 NIC liability for 2021/22 is:

£	158	.	60

The Class 4 NIC liability for 2021/22 is:

£	293	.	58

The total NIC liability for 2021/22 is:

£	452	.	18

Working

	£
Profits	12,830
Less lower profits limit	(9,568)
Excess	3,262

Class 4 NICs (9% × £3,262) = £293.58

Class 2 NICs = £3.05 × 52 = £158.60

Total NICs £(299.70+158.60) = **£452.18**

Task 6.2

The Class 2 NIC liability for **2021/22** is:

£	158	.	60

The Class 4 NIC liability for **2021/22** is:

£	3,817	.	78

The total NIC liability for **2021/22** is:

£	3,976	.	38

Working

	£
Upper profits limit	50,270
Less: lower profits limit	(9,568)
Excess	40,702

	£
Class 4 NICs (9% × £40,702)	3,663.18
+ 2% × £(58,000 – 50,270)	154.60
	3817.78

Class 2 NICs = £3.05 × 52 = £158.60

Total NICs £(3,817.78+ 158.60) = **£3976.38**

Task 6.3

The Class 2 NIC liability for 2021/22 is:

£	0	.	0

The Class 4 NIC liability for 2021/22 is:

£	0	.	0

The total NIC liability for 2021/22 is:

£	0	.	0

As Raj's trading profits are below the lower profits limit, there is no liability to Class 4 NICs. There is also no liability to Class 2 NICs because his profits are below the small profits threshold of £6,515.

Task 6.4

The Class 2 NIC liability for 2021/22 is:

£	158	.	60

The Class 4 NIC liability for 2021/22 is:

£	4,257	.	78

The total NIC liability for 2021/22 is:

£	4,416	.	38

Working

Class 2 = £3.05 × 52 = £158.60

		£
Class 4	£(50,270 – 9,568) × 9% (main)	3,663.18
	£(80,000 – 50,270) × 2% (additional)	594.60
		4,257.78

Total NICs £(4,257.78 + 158.60) = **£4416.38**

ANSWERS

Task 6.5

(a) The share of profits taxable on Paula for 2021/22 is:

£	14,000

Working

Share of profits for y/e 31.12.22 is £280,000 × 20% = £56,000
Basis period for 2021/22 = 1.1.22 to 5.4.22 (3/12 × £56,000 = £14,000)

and for 2022/23 is:

£	56,000

Working

Basis period for 2022/23 = 1.1.22 to 31.12.22

and the overlap profits to carry forward are:

£	14,000

Working

1.1.22 to 5.4.22 (3/12 × £56,000 = £14,000)

(b) The Class 4 National Insurance Contributions payable by Paula for 2021/22 are:

£	398	.	88

Working

£(14,000 – 9,568) = £4,432 × 9%

Task 6.6

Class 4 NICs	£
Class 4 NICs at 9% (£50,270 - £9,568) × 9%	3,663.18
Class 4 NICs at 2% (£62,000- £50,270) × 2%	234.60
Total Class 4 NICs due	3,897.78

Make sure you look carefully at how you are asked to present the figures. In earlier Tasks you were only asked to give the total Class 4 NIC figure but you may be asked to show the amounts chargeable at 9% and 2% as in this Task.

Task 6.7

£136

	£
Class 2 contributions 14 × £3.05	43
Class 4 contributions £(10,600 – 9,568) × 9%	93
Total contributions	136

Task 6.8

£3,721

	£
£(53,150 – 50,270) = 2,880 @ 2%	58
£(50,270 – 9,568) = 40,702 @ 9%	3,663
Class 4 NIC payable	3,721

The answer £3,674 uses the accruals basis rather than the profits for the year ended 31 May 2021. The answer £3,922 uses a rate of 9% throughout. The answer £3,663 is just the amount chargeable at 9%.

Task 6.9

£3,858

	£
£(60,000 – 50,270) = 9,730 × 2%	195
£(50,270 – 9,568) = 40,702 × 9%	3,663
Class 4 contributions	3,858

Class 4 NICs are based on the trading profits for the period of account ending in the tax year.

Chapter 7 – Computing corporation tax

Task 7.1

	£	£
Profit per accounts		656,980
	Add	Deduct
Depreciation charge	83,420	0
Qualifying charitable donation	1,900	0
Gifts to customers	900	0
Accountancy and audit fee	0	0
Legal fees – renewal of 20 year lease (N1)	0	0
Legal fees – issue of debenture	0	0
Repairs – knocked down wall (N2)	0	0
Initial repairs to office	12,200	0
Other expenses	0	0
Debenture interest (Investment income)	0	(24,700)
Bank interest (Investment income)	0	(4,800)
Dividends	0	(56,000)
Capital allowances	0	(13,200)
Interest payable on trading loans	0	0
Net adjustments		(280)
Taxable trading profit		656,700

Notes.

1 The costs of renewing a short lease and of obtaining loan finance for trading purposes are allowable.

2 The replacement of the wall is allowable since the whole structure is not being replaced. The repairs to the office building are not allowable, being capital in nature, as the building was not in a usable state when purchased and this was reflected in the purchase price.

Task 7.2

	Allow ✓	Disallow and add back ✓	Not taxable as trading income so deduct ✓
Dividends received from an unconnected company			✓
Profit on sale of shares			✓
Running costs of car with 20% private use by an employee	✓		
Parking fine of director		✓	
Capital allowances	✓		
Director's salary	✓		
Bank interest received			✓

Task 7.3

	Year to 31 December 2021 £	Five months to 31 May 2022 £
Trading profits	352,941	147,059
Property business income	10,800	4,500
Chargeable gain	0	3,000
Qualifying charitable donations paid	-30,000	-40,000
Taxable total profits	333,741	114,559

Tutor's notes

1 Trading profits are time apportioned.
2 Property business income is on an accruals basis.
3 Chargeable gains are allocated to the period in which they are realised.
4 Qualifying charitable donations are allocated to the period in which they are paid.

Task 7.4

	Time apportioned ✓	Period in which arises ✓	Separate computation ✓
Capital allowances			✓
Trading income	✓		
Property income		✓	
Investment income		✓	
Chargeable gain		✓	

Task 7.5

The corporation tax payable by Rosemary Ltd for period ended 31 March 2022 is:

£	171,000

Working

	£
Trading profits	600,000
Property business income	300,000
Taxable total profits	900,000

Note. Dividends are not included as part of taxable total profits.

FY21	£
£900,000 × 19%	171,000

Task 7.6

	£
Trading profits after capital allowances	376,200
Investment income	12,000
Property income	8,000
Chargeable gain	22,000
Qualifying charitable donations	-6,000
Taxable total profit	412,200
Corporation tax liability	78,318

Task 7.7

A company usually pays corporation tax on dividend income.

	✓
True	
False	✓

Task 7.8

	✓
When a company has a long period of account, it prepares two tax computations for the period. The first one being for the first twelve months and the second being for the balance.	✓
When a company has a long period of account, the trading profits after capital allowances are prorated.	
When a company has a long period of account, the qualifying charitable donations are allocated to the period in which they accrue.	
A company can prepare a tax computation for a maximum period of 18 months.	

Task 7.9

The corporation tax payable by Tarragon Ltd for period ended 31 March 2022 is:

£	49,400

Working

	£
Taxable trading profits	200,000
Property income	50,000
Investment income	10,000
Taxable total profits	260,000

Note. Dividends are not included as part of taxable total profits. Dividends paid are not tax deductible.

FY21	£
£260,000 × 19%	49,400

ANSWERS

Chapter 8 – Losses

Task 8.1

	2019/20 £	2020/21 £	2021/22 £	2022/23 £
Trading profits	12,000	0	8,000	14,000
Trading loss offset against future year	0	0	(8,000)	(3,600)
Property income	10,400	11,000	11,000	11,000
Trading loss offset against current year	0	(11,000)	0	0
Trading loss offset against previous year	(22,400)	0	0	0
Net income	0	0	11,000	21,400

Task 8.2

	✓
True	
False	✓

An individual cannot restrict a claim to set a trading loss against total income in order to have enough net income to use his personal allowance – the loss must be set-off as far as possible even if this means that the personal allowance is not available.

Task 8.3

	✓
True	
False	✓

An individual does not have to make a trading loss claim against total income in the tax year of the loss before making a claim to set the loss against total income in the preceding year – a claim can be made for either year or both years, and in any order.

Task 8.4

	✓
True	✓
False	

An individual can only carry a trading loss forward against trading income of the same trade.

Task 8.5

(a)

	Year ended 31 March		
	2020 £	2021 £	2022 £
Trading profits	62,000	20,000	0
Investment income	1,200	600	1,200
Total profits	63,200	20,600	1,200
Current period loss relief	0	0	(1,200)
Carry back loss relief	0	(20,600)	0
Total profits after loss relief	63,200	0	0
Qualifying charitable donation	(100)	0	0
Taxable total profits	63,100	0	0

(b) The trading loss available to carry forward at 31 March 2022 is:

£	61,200

Working

(£83,000 – £1,200 – £20,600)

Task 8.6

(a)

	Year ended 30.6.19 £	9 months to 31.3.20 £	Year ended 31.3.21 £	Year ended 31.3.22 £
Trading profits	6,200	4,320	0	53,000
Investment income	80	240	260	200
Property income	1,420	1,440	1,600	1,500
Chargeable gains	0	7,680	0	0
Total profits	7,700	13,680	1,860	54,700
Current period loss relief	0	0	(1,860)	0
Carry back loss relief	(1,925)	(13,680)	0	0
Carry forward loss relief				(54,700)
Total profits after loss relief	5,775	0	0	0
Qualifying charitable donation	(1,000)	0	0	0
Taxable total profits	4,775	0	0	0

Tutor's note. The loss can be carried back to set against profits arising in the previous 12 months. This means that the set-off in the y/e 30.6.19 is restricted to 3/12 × £7,700 = £1,925. When a loss is carried forward, a claim must be made to specify the amount of loss relieved.

(b) The trading loss available to carry forward at 31 March 2022 is:

£	27,835

Working

(£100,000 – £1,860 – £13,680 – £1,925 – £54,700)

(c) The capital loss available to carry forward at 31 March 2022 is:

£	9,423

Task 8.7

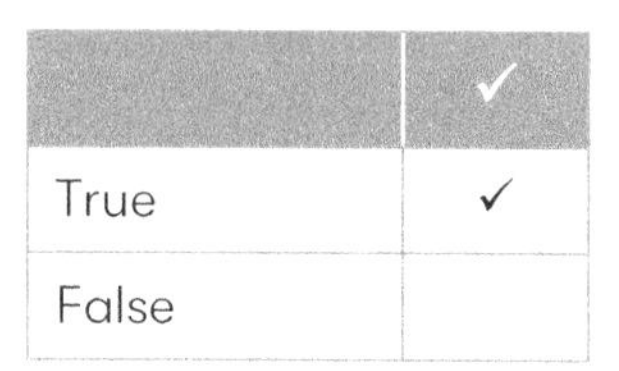

	✓
True	✓
False	

A company must offset its trading loss against total profits in the loss-making period before carrying the loss back.

Task 8.8

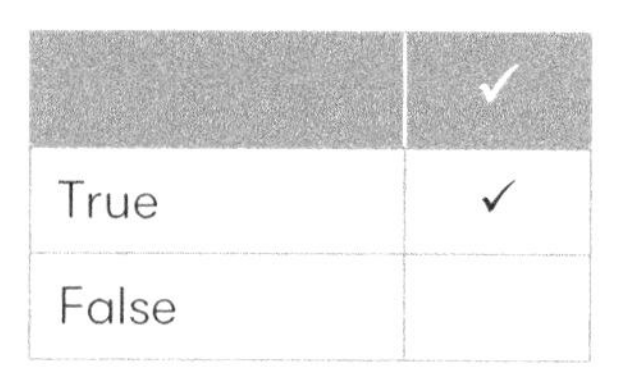

	✓
True	✓
False	

If a company carries a trading loss forward, the company can choose how much of the loss is to be set against total profits so as not to waste any qualifying donations.

Task 8.9

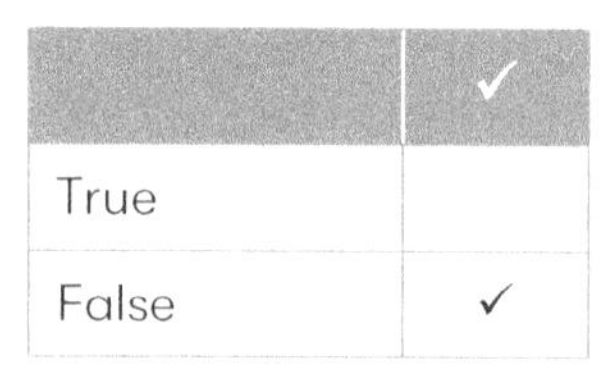

	✓
True	
False	✓

A company can set-off a capital loss against capital gains only.

Task 8.10

	True ✓	False ✓
When a company ceases trading, trading losses incurred in the 36 months prior to cessation can be carried back 12 months.		✓
Losses offset under terminal loss relief for companies are offset against the company's total profits (before QCDs)	✓	
Losses offset under terminal loss relief are on a FIFO basis		✓
Losses offset under terminal loss relief for sole traders are offset against the individual's trading profits only	✓	
Opening year loss relief is available to both companies and individuals		✓
Losses offset under opening year loss relief for sole traders are offset on a LIFO basis		✓
Losses offset under opening year loss relief for sole traders are offset against the individual's total income	✓	

Where a company ceases trading, terminal loss relief is available for losses incurred in the 12 months prior to cessation. Losses can be carried back to the preceding 36 months.

Losses offset under terminal loss relief for sole traders (and companies) are on a LIFO basis

Opening year loss relief is only available to individuals

Losses offset under opening year loss relief for sole traders are offset on a FIFO basis

---

Task 8.11

Sally

Sally's 2021/22 trading loss is £10,000.

Sally is an ongoing partner and can therefore make a current year (2021/22) and or prior year (2020/21) claim against her total income.

Her total income in the current year (2021/22) is her property income of £15,000. Offsetting the £10,000 of trade loss against the property income would save some tax at 20% and waste some personal allowance thus saving no additional tax.

A prior year (2020/21) claim against total income would offset the £10,000 trade loss against Sally's total income of £36,000 (1/2 × £42,000 + £15,000). The £10,000 trade loss offset would all save tax at 20%.

If no claim is made then Sally's trade loss would be automatically carried forward and offset against the £10,000 of trade profits she will generate in 2022/23. As Sally would still have £15,000 property income, this trade profit would have been taxed at 20% and so an offset would save 20% tax but there would be later tax relief (ie no repayment generated).

It is recommended that Sally make a prior year claim to offset the trade loss against her total income of £36,000 in 2020/21. This would save the most tax whilst generating a cashflow advantage as she would be able to get a refund of her tax paid.

Sara

Sara's 2021/22 trading loss is £10,000.

Like Sally, she can make a current year (2021/22) and or prior year (2020/21) claim against her total income. She has no other income in 2021/22 so no claim is valid. In 2020/21 her only income was her share of the trade profits of £21,000. An offset would mainly save her tax at 20% but would waste some personal allowance.

As Sara is ceasing to trade a carry forward offset will not be possible. However, her £10,000 trade loss will be a terminal loss and so can be carried back three years on a LIFO basis against trade profits only. This claim would have the same effect as the prior year offset outlined above.

Sara would be indifferent between making a terminal loss claim and a prior year offset against total income.

Jo

Jo's 2021/22 trading loss is £10,000.

Like Sally and Sara, she can make a current year and or prior year claim against her total income. In 2021/22 she has no other income so a current year claim is not possible.

In 2020/21 Jo's total income consisted of her salary of £160,000. A £10,000 trade loss offset would save her tax at 45% as an additional rate taxpayer.

In addition, as Jo has made a trade loss in her first tax year, she can carry her trade loss back three years on a FIFO basis against her total income. This would allow her to carry back her loss to 2018/19 total income of £160,000 also saving her tax at 45%.

Jo should make the opening year loss claim to carry her loss back to 2018/19. While this saves the same amount of tax as a prior year loss offset it leaves more income available to carry back against if the partnership were to continue to make a loss in her early years as a partner.

Task 8.12

(a) **Identify whether the following statements are true or false.**

	True ✓	False ✓
Osian can claim to use his loss of 2021/22 against his total income in 2020/21 only, in order to preserve his personal allowance in 2021/22.	✓	
Osian can claim to use his loss of 2021/22 against his trading income in 2020/21 only, in order to preserve his personal allowance in 2021/22. • A prior year claim is against total income not trading income.		✓
Osian must claim to use his loss of 2021/22 against his total income in 2021/22, before being able to carry it back. • A sole trader can offset their trade loss in the current year and/ or prior year in any order.		✓

(b) **Identify whether the following statements are true or false for a company.**

	True ✓	False ✓
When a trading loss is carried back by a company, it is set-off after deducting qualifying charitable donations. • It is set off against total profits ie before QCDs.		✓
A company can carry a trade loss back 12 months against total profits and forward 36 months against profits of the same trade. • The carry forward of trade losses is indefinite and against total profits.		✓
A company must set-off trading losses in the current period before carrying back to the previous period.	✓	

ANSWERS

Chapter 9 – Self assessment for individuals

Task 9.1

	✓
31 January 2023	✓
5 April 2023	
31 October 2022	
31 December 2022	

The date is given in your reference material.

Task 9.2

	✓
The full amount of £20,500 will be paid on 31 January 2023.	
Payments on account based on the estimated 2021/22 liability will be made on 31 January and 31 July 2022, with the balance payable on 31 January 2023.	
Payments on account of £10,250 will be made on 31 January and 31 July 2022 with nothing due on 31 January 2023.	
Payments on account of £7,250 will be made on 31 January and 31 July 2022, with the balance of £6,000 being paid on 31 January 2023.	✓

Details about payment of income tax are given in your reference material.

Task 9.3

	✓
100%	
50%	✓
35%	
15%	

This penalty is given in your reference material.

Task 9.4

	✓
True	✓
False	

The return is filed less than 3 months after the due filing date. This penalty is given in your reference material.

Task 9.5

	✓
True	✓
False	

The penalty for failure to keep records is £3,000 per tax year or accounting period and is given in your reference material.

Task 9.6

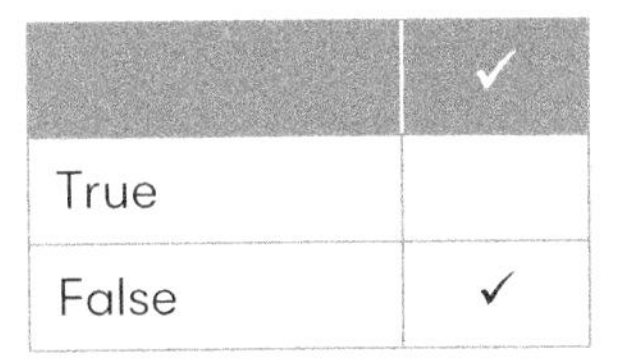

	✓
True	
False	✓

Penalties for late payment do not apply to payments on account.

Task 9.7

05/10/2022

The deadline is 5 October following the end of the tax year and is stated in your reference material.

Task 9.8

Penalty	£
Fixed penalty	100
Daily penalty	900
Tax-geared penalty	300

22/10/2023

This information is given to you in the reference material.

Task 9.9

31/01/2028

The deadline is five years from the filing deadline and is stated in your reference material.

Chapter 10 – Self assessment for companies

Task 10.1

Instalment	Due date (xx/xx/xxxx)	Amount due £
1	14/10/2021	125,000
2	14/01/2022	125,000
3	14/04/2022	125,000
4	14/07/2022	125,000

Task 10.2

	True ✓	False ✓
A company with a period of account ending on 31 March 2022 must keep its records until 31 March 2024.		✓ (until 31 March 2028)
An individual who becomes chargeable to income tax in 2021/22 must notify HMRC by 31 October 2022.		✓ (by 5 October 2022)
A large company will not have to pay corporation tax by instalments if it has profits not exceeding £10m and was not large in the previous accounting period.	✓	
A company which is not large (for corporation tax purposes) must pay its corporation tax by nine months and one day after the end of its accounting period.	✓	

Task 10.3

The corporation tax return must be filed by:

28/02/2023

The corporation tax return must be filed by:

30/06/2022

Task 10.4

A company must keep its accounting records for six years. Failure to do so may incur a penalty of £ 3,000.

Task 10.5

The penalty for late filing is

£	200

The return was due within 12 months from the end of the period of account ie 31 March 2023. It was therefore 4 months late and the penalty is fixed at £200.

Task 10.6

HMRC must give notice by 30/06/2023 .

The deadline is within 12 months from the actual filing date.

Task 10.7

£100

There is a £100 penalty for late return which is submitted within three months of the due date (ie filing due by 30 September 2022 - 12 months after the end of the period to which the return relates).

Task 10.8

The returns for the year ended 31 December 2021 and the period ended 31 March 2022 must both be filed by 31 March 2023.

Task 10.9

Unincorporated businesses have penalties for late filing of returns, late payment of tax and late notification of chargeability whereas companies only have penalties for late filing and notification of chargeability.

Chapter 11 – Chargeable gains for companies

Task 11.1

	£
Proceeds	230,000
Less cost	(160,000)
Unindexed gain	70,000
Less indexation allowance 0.535 × £160,000 (restricted)	(70,000)
Chargeable gain/allowable loss	0

Task 11.2

	£
Proceeds	180,000
Less: cost	(100,000)
enhancement expenditure	(25,000)
Unindexed gain	55,000
Less: indexation allowance on cost 0.407 × £100,000	(40,700)
indexation allowance on enhancement 0.280 × £25,000	(7,000)
Chargeable gain	7,300

Task 11.3

	✓
True	
False	✓

Individuals are entitled to an annual exempt amount but not companies.

Task 11.4

(a) The gain on disposal in May 2018 was:

£	67,000

Working

	£
Proceeds	145,000
Less cost	(50,000)
	95,000
Less indexation allowance 0.560 × £50,000	(28,000)
Chargeable gain	**67,000**

(b) The gain available for rollover relief is:

£	62,000

Working

	£
Gain	67,000
Less chargeable in 2018	
Proceeds not reinvested = £(145,000 – 140,000)	(5,000)
Gain available for rollover relief	**62,000**

(c) The base cost of the property acquired in April 2021 is:

£	78,000

Working

	£
Cost of new property	140,000
Less gain rolled over	(62,000)
Base cost of new property	**78,000**

Task 11.5

	✓
The start of the previous accounting period and the end of the next accounting period	
Three years before and three years after the date of the disposal	
One year before and three years after the date of the disposal	✓
One year before and one year after the date of the disposal	

Task 11.6

	True ✓	False ✓
If an asset is bought by a company prior to December 2017, indexation allowance will be available on disposal at a gain.	✓	
Indexation on subsequent capital enhancement expenditure by a company must be calculated separately to the indexation on the original cost.	✓	
No deduction is available for any legal fees associated with the sale of a chargeable asset. • Relief for incidental costs of disposal is available.		✓
Indexation allowance can create a loss. • Indexation cannot create or increase a loss		✓
Where only three quarters of a building is used for trading purposes, rollover relief is maximised by reinvesting the whole of the proceeds in a replacement asset. • Only three quarters of the proceeds on the sale of the building would need to be reinvested for full rollover relief to be available.		✓
To qualify for rollover relief both the original asset and replacement asset must fall within the same category of qualifying asset. • The assets both need to qualify for rollover relief but do not need to be in the same category.		✓
The reinvestment needs to take place in the three years before or 12 months after the disposal of the original asset. • The reinvestment is in the 12 months before or three years after the disposal of the original asset.		✓

Task 11.7

(a) Edline Ltd's gain on the disposal before rollover relief is:

£	65,000

Working

	£
Proceeds	125,000
Less cost	(60,000)
Gain	**65,000**

(b) Assuming rollover relief is claimed, the gain immediately chargeable is:

£	1,500

Proceeds not re-invested (£125,000 – £123,500)

(c) The gain which Edline Ltd can rollover into the new premises is:

£	£63,500

Working

	£
Gain	65,000
Less immediately chargeable	(1,500)
Gain rolled-over against new premises	63,500

ANSWERS

Chapter 12 – Share disposals

Task 12.1

FA 1985 pool

	No. of shares	Original cost £	Indexed cost £
September 2001			
Acquisition	5,000	10,000	10,000
October 2004			
Indexed rise 0.080 × £10,000			800
Rights 1:5 @ £5	1,000	5,000	5,000
	6,000	15,000	15,800
August 2006			
Indexed rise 0.056 × £15,800			885
Acquisition	14,000	84,000	84,000
	20,000	99,000	100,685
January 2022			
Indexed rise 0.396 × £100,685			39,871
			140,556
Sale (99,000/140,556 × 18,000/20,000)	(18,000)	(89,100)	(126,500)
c/f	2,000	9,900	14,056

Gain

	£
Proceeds	155,000
Less cost	(89,100)
	65,900
Less indexation allowance £(126,500 – 89,100)	(37,400)
Chargeable gain	28,500

Task 12.2

FA 1985 pool

	No. of shares	Original cost £	Indexed cost £
26 May 1995			
Acquisition	4,000	24,000	24,000
30 June 1996 Bonus issue (1/2 × 4,000)	2,000		
24 October 2003			
Indexed rise 0.221 × £24,000			5,304
Acquisition	5,000	27,500	27,500
c/f	11,000	51,500	56,804
25 May 2021			
Indexed rise 0.523 × £56,804			29,708
			86,512
Disposal	(11,000)	(51,500)	(86,512)
c/f	0	0	0

Gain

	£
Proceeds	78,200
Less cost	(51,500)
	26,700
Less indexation allowance £(86,512 – 51,500)	(35,012)
Gain	Nil

Task 12.3

	✓
True	✓
False	

Indexation allowance on rights issue shares runs from the date of the rights issue even though the rights issue shares are treated as having been acquired at the time of the original acquisition to which they relate.

ANSWERS

Task 12.4

£	6,186

	£
Proceeds	53,400
Less cost	(36,800)
	16,600
Less indexation allowance to December 2017 0.283 × £36,800	(10,414)
Gain	6,186

£	14,982

	No. of shares	Indexed cost
		£
Acquisition	16,000	32,000
Indexed rise to December 2017		
0.244 × £32,000		7,808
		39,808
Disposal	(10,000)	(24,880)
	6,000	14,928

The answer £12,000 is the unindexed pool of cost immediately after the sale. The answer £39,808 is the indexed cost of the pool immediately before the disposal. The answer £24,880 is the amount of indexed cost used on the disposal.

Task 12.5

(a)

	Number of shares	Cost £	Indexed cost £
1 March 2012 - purchase	5,000	21,000	21,000
Sep 2014 - 1 for 2 bonus issue	2,500		
Indexation Mar 12 – Dec 17			
0.155 × £21,000			3,255
Aug 18 Acquisition	4,000	30,000	30,000
	11,500	51,000	54,255
Sep 21 Disposal	(1,000)	(4,435)	(4,718)
Pool c/f	10,500	46,565	49,537

(b)

	£
Previous 9 days sale- 1,000 shares bought 8 Sep 21	
Proceeds (1,000 × £8.60)	8,600
Cost (1,000 × £8.00)	(8,000)
Gain	600
FA85 share pool	
Proceeds (1,000 × £8.60)	8,600
Cost	(4,435)
Indexation allowances (£4,718 - £4,435)	(283)
Gain	3,882
Total gains (£600 + £3,882)	4,482

ANSWERS

Chapter 13 – Business Disposals

Task 13.1

	✓
£33,300	✓
£38,300	
£45,600	
£50,600	

Working

	£
Proceeds of sale	90,600
Less cost	(40,000)
Less enhancement expenditure	(5,000)
Chargeable gain	45,600
Less annual exempt amount	(12,300)
Taxable gain	33,300

Task 13.2

Jack would pay capital gains tax at:

20%

Gains are subject to capital gains tax at 10% (for basic rate taxpayers) and 20% (for higher and additional rate taxpayers).

Task 13.3

Gayle's capital gains tax liability for 2021/22 is:

£	1,260

Working

	£
Chargeable gains (£3,000 + £18,100)	21,100
Less annual exempt amount	(12,300)
Taxable gains	8,800

CGT payable

	£
£5,000 @ 10%	500
£3,800 @ 20%	760
	1,260

Task 13.4

Gerry's capital gains tax liability for 2021/22 is:

£	1,811

Working

	£
Chargeable gains	27,100
Less annual exempt amount	(12,300)
Taxable gains	14,800

CGT	£
£11,495 (W) @ 10%	1,150
£3,305 @ 20%	661
	1,811
(W) Unused basic rate band is £37,700 – £26,205 = £11,495	

Task 13.5

	£	£
Proceeds of goodwill	50,000	
Less cost	0	
Gain/(loss) on goodwill		50,000
Proceeds of shop	90,000	
Less cost	(80,000)	
Gain/(loss) on shop		10,000
Proceeds of warehouse	130,000	
Less cost	(150,000)	
Gain/(loss) on warehouse		(20,000)
Net gains eligible for business asset disposal relief		40,000
Less annual exempt amount		(12,300)
Taxable gains		27,700
CGT payable		2,770

Task 13.6

	✓
True	✓
False	

The lifetime limit of gains eligible for business asset disposal relief is £1,000,000.

Task 13.7

The taxable gain arising on the sale of the Blue Ltd shares is:

£	137,700

Working

	£	£
Proceeds		200,000
Less cost	65,000	
Less gain rolled over	(15,000)	
		(50,000)
Chargeable gain		150,000
Less annual exempt amount		(12,300)
Taxable gain		**137,700**

Task 13.8

(a) Fran's chargeable gain on her disposal is:

£	0

Working

	£
Proceeds (MV) June 2021	500,000
Less cost	(75,000)
Gain	425,000
Less gift relief	(425,000)
Gain left in charge	0

(b) Anna's chargeable gain (before deduction of the annual exempt amount) on her disposal is:

£	445,000

Working

	£	£
Proceeds July 2022		520,000
Cost (MV)	500,000	
Less gift relief gain (from above)	(425,000)	
Base cost		(75,000)
Chargeable gain		**445,000**

Task 13.9

	True	False
Business asset disposal relief will be available on the disposal of a 6% shareholding in L Ltd, an unquoted trading company which has been held for three years. The shareholder has worked for the company for five years - This statement correctly meets the conditions for BADR. See reference material available in your assessment for the conditions.	✓	
Business asset disposal relief will be available on the disposal of a 6% shareholding in L Ltd, an unquoted investment company which has been held for three years. The shareholder has worked for the company for five years – The company must be a trading company to qualify for BADR.		✓
Gains of £2 million on disposal of a business owned for five years are taxed at 10%. - There is a lifetime limit for gains which qualify for BADR of £1 million. So it isn't true that **all** £2 million of gains would be taxed at 10%.		✓

Task 13.10

Asset	Market value £	Original cost £	TWDV £	Impact
Factory	95,000	110,000		Capital loss
Warehouse	95,000	80,000		Chargeable gain
Plant & machinery	1,000	10,000	5,000	Decrease trading profit
Goodwill	32,000	0		Chargeable gain
Inventory	8,000	6,000		Increase trading profit

Task 13.11

(a)

Taxable gain	£
Gain on factory (£300,000- £220,000)	80,000
Loss on warehouse (£100,000 - £105,0000)	(5,000)
Gain on goodwill (£96,000 - £0)	96,000
Less annual exempt amount (already used)	0
Taxable gain	171,000

(b)

Tax charged on the gain	£
Taxable gain	171,000
CGT @ 10% (BADR)	17,100

(c)

	£
Proceeds	536,000
Add income tax and NIC saved on adjustments (given)	940
Less capital gains tax on gains @ 10% (b)	(17,100)
Post-tax proceeds	519,840

Task 13.12

Calculate Paul's taxable gain from the sale of his shares.

£	387,700

Taxable gains	£
Proceeds	420,000
Cost	(20,000)
Chargeable gain	400,000
Less AEA	(12,300)
Taxable gains	387,700
CGT @ 10% (BADR) × £100,000	10,000
CGT @ 20% (£387,700 - £100,000)	57,540
Total CGT	67,540

Calculate the tax that will be charged on Paul's taxable gains assuming all beneficial claims are made.

£	67,540

Calculate Paul's after-tax proceeds from the sale of his shares.

£	352,460

	£
Proceeds	420,000
Less capital gains tax on gain @ 10%/ 20%	(67,540)
After-tax proceeds	352,460

ANSWERS

Chapter 14 - Tax Planning for Businesses

Task 14.1

From:	AAT student
To:	A Client
Date:	Today
Subject:	Badges of trade

In order to decide whether a trade is being carried on the following 'badges of trade' need to be considered:

(a) **Subject matter.** When people engage in trade, they frequently do so by purchasing and re-selling objects with a view to making a profit. Objects bought for this purpose are often not the type of objects that would be bought for investment or enjoyment. This means that the subject matter of a transaction will very often indicate whether a trade is being carried on or not.

(b) **Length of ownership.** A short period of ownership is an indication of an intention to trade in a commodity.

(c) **Frequency of transactions.** Where the same type of article is repeatedly bought and sold, it will normally suggest that there is trading in that article.

(d) **Supplementary work** on or in connection with the property sold, eg modification, processing, packaging, or renovating the item sold suggests the carrying on of a trade.

(e) **Acquisition of asset.** If goods are acquired deliberately, trading may be indicated. If goods are acquired by gift or inheritance, their later sale is unlikely to constitute trading.

(f) **Profit motive.** This is usually the most important consideration though its absence does not prevent a trade being carried on if, in fact, the operation is run on commercial lines and a profit does result.

(g) **Existence of similar trading transactions or interests.** If the seller of the goods also carries out other similar trading transactions, it will normally suggest that the sale of the goods is trading.

(h) **The source of finance.** If an asset is acquired with short term finance or its disposal is necessary to repay the borrowed funds, it is likely that there is a trade.

(i) **Reason for sale.** If an asset is sold for profit purposes then it is likely that a trade is being carried on. If an asset is sold for other reasons, for example a change in personal circumstances or a cash flow emergency, it would be an indicator that a trade is not being carried out.

These **badges of trade** are only general indications and, in each case, all the facts must be considered before any decision can be made.

Task 14.2

	Trade ✓
The number of transactions	✓
Interval of time between purchase and sale	
Changes to the asset	✓
Correction of own work	

Interval of time between purchase and sale – a short length of ownership would indicate trade.

Correction of own work – this is not one of the badges of trade.

Task 14.3

(a) **If Sarah continues as a sole trader**

Sarah will pay income tax on her trade profits of £50,000. The first £37,700 of these profits will be taxed at 20% with the excess at 40%.

In addition, Sarah will pay Class 2 and Class 4 NICs. The Class 2 NIC will be £158.60. (£3.05 × 52) and the Class 4 NIC will be £3,638.88. ((£50,000 - £9,568) × 9%))

She is taxed on her trade profits before any drawings are deducted so her extraction of profits will not change her tax position.

If Sarah forms a company

If Sarah forms a company, it will pay corporation tax on its taxable total profits and the choice of how she extracts her profits impacts the tax position.

Corporation tax for her company

The company will pay corporation tax at 19% on the trade profits of £50,000 less the salary of £30,000 less employer's NIC on the salary. The employer's NIC will be at 13.8% on the salary in excess of £8,840. No employment allowance is available as Sarah is the sole director and shareholder of the company.

Tax on Sarah

Sarah will pay income tax on her salary of £30,000 and dividends of £10,000. The £30,000 salary all falls in the basic rate band and will be taxed at 20%. £7,700 of the dividend income also falls in the basic rate band of tax being taxed at 7.5% with the balance in the higher rate band being taxed at 32.5%.

There will be employee's NIC at 12% on the salary in excess of £9,568. There is no NIC on dividends.

(b) The relatively high tax cost of Sarah incorporating her business arises because of her salary attracting both employee and employer NICs.

Restricting the salary to around £8,000 and taxing a correspondingly higher amount of dividends, would significantly reduce her overall tax cost.

Task 14.4

	True ✓	False ✓
Employer's NIC will be due at 13.8% on any salary paid in excess of £9,568. • Employer's NIC is due on salary over £8,840		✓
Dividends paid are not tax deductible for the company.	✓	
An additional rate tax payer will pay income tax at 32.5% on any dividend income received. • The rate is 38.1% for an additional rate tax payer.		✓
Any salary and employee's NICs thereon are tax deductible for the company. • It is the salary and employer's NIC that are tax deductible for a company.		✓
A company with a single director and no other employees is not entitled to the £4,000 employment allowance.	✓	

Task 14.5

	True ✓	False ✓
A sole trader is a separate legal entity • It is a company that is a separate legal entity.		✓
Incorporated businesses must follow more rules and regulations	✓	
The employment allowance is available to a partnership. • The employment allowance is available to any business that employs staff regardless of whether the business is incorporated or not. (But it is not available to a company with a single director and no other employees). It is offset against the businesses employer's Class 1 NIC liability not against the owners Class 2 & 4 NICs.	✓	
A sole trader pays income tax and employee's NIC on their profits. • A sole trade pays income tax and Class 2 and 4 NICs (not employee's NICs)		✓
Companies can take a corporation tax deduction for any salary and employer's NIC.	✓	

Task 14.6

If Matilda chose to extract her profits by way of the maximum possible dividend , what dividend would she receive?

£	162,000

How much post-tax cash would Matilda receive if she extracted the maximum possible dividend?

£	100,278

	£
Tilly Ltd's TTP	200,000
Less corporation tax @ 19%	(38,000)
Profits available to distribute as a dividend = dividend	162,000
As an additional rate taxpayer, Matilda will suffer 38.1%% income tax on this dividend with no NIC. (38.1% × £162,000)	(61,722)
After-tax dividend kept by Matilda	100,278

If Matilda chose to extract her profits by way of the maximum salary, what salary would she receive?

£	175,747

How much post-tax cash would Matilda receive if she extracted the maximum possible salary?

£	93,146

	£
Tilly Ltd's TTP	200,000
Employer's NIC will be due at 13.8% on any salary that Matilda chooses to take from the company. So, the TTP figures represents 113.8% of the salary. Employer's NIC on salary to withdraw (13.8/113.8 × £200,000) (Note)	(24,253)
Salary for Matilda to withdraw (100/113.8 × £200,000)	175,747
This salary will be taxed on Matilda, an additional rate taxpayer, at a rate of 45% income tax and 2% employee's NICs. Thus 47% tax will be suffered (47% × £175,747)	(82,601)
After tax salary kept by Matilda	93,146

As Matilda is the sole director and employee of the company, there is no employment allowance available.

Task 14.7

C 20% Anne, 80% Vlad

The couple's income tax liability will be minimised by Anne taking the lower share of the profit (as the additional rate tax payer) and Vlad taking the lower profit share due to having some personal allowance left unused and then only being a basic rate tax payer.

Task 14.8

When an asset is passed between a married couple/ civil partners the asset transfers at nil gain/ nil loss for capital gains tax purposes.

AAT AQ2022
ASSESSMENT 1
Business Tax

Time allowed: 2 hours

You are advised to attempt the AAT practice/sample assessment 1 online from the AAT website. This will ensure you are prepared for how the assessment will be presented on the AAT's system when you attempt the real assessment. Please access the assessment using the address below:

https://www.aat.org.uk/training/study-support/search

AAT AQ2022
PRACTICE ASSESSMENT 1

AAT AQ2022
ASSESSMENT 2
Business Tax

Time allowed: 2 hours

You are advised to attempt the assessment 2 online from the AAT website. This will ensure you are prepared for how the assessment will be presented on the AAT's system when you attempt the real assessment. Please access the assessment using the address below:

https://www.aat.org.uk/training/study-support/search

AAT AQ2022
PRACTICE ASSESSMENT 2

BPP PRACTICE ASSESSMENT 1
BUSINESS TAX

Time allowed: 2 hours

PRACTICE ASSESSMENT 1

Business Tax (BSTX)
BPP practice assessment 1

In the live assessment you will have access to the Tax tables and reference material which have been reproduced at the back of this Question Bank. Please use them whilst completing this practice assessment so that you are familiar with their content.

Task 1 (8 marks)

This task is about adjusting accounting profits and losses for tax purposes.

The statement of profit or loss for George Checkers shows the following:

	£	£
Gross profit		396,550
General expenses (see notes below)	85,480	
Irrecoverable debts (see notes below)	585	
Motor expenses (see notes below)	7,880	
Wages and salaries	54,455	
Depreciation charge	21,080	
		(169,480)
Profit for the year		227,070

Notes.

General expenses include		£
Gifts to customers – Christmas cakes costing £4.50 each		1,350
Building a new wall around car park		2,200

Irrecoverable debts are made up of:		£
Trade debts written-off		350
Increase in general provision		400
Trade debts recovered		(165)
		585

Motor expenses are made up of:	Private usage %	Annual expense £
George	25	6,600
Salesman	20	1,280

Capital allowances:		£
Capital allowances have been calculated as		15,000

Calculate the taxable trading profit for George Checkers by entering adjustments to accounting profit below. If no adjustment is required, you should enter a zero. If any adjustments are deducted from accounting profits, these should be shown as a negative figure (for example, a deduction of 5,000 should be shown as -5000 or -5,000). (8 marks)

	£
Accounting profit	227,070
Gifts to customers Must have logo No food or drink	1350
New wall Capital	2200
Irrecoverable debts only specific allowed	400
Motor expenses – George	1650
Motor expenses – Salesman	0
Wages and salaries	0
Depreciation dealt with CA	21080
Capital allowances	(15,000)
Taxable profit	AUTOSUM

238,750

Task 2 (12 marks)

This task is about capital allowances.

Mr Wish commenced trade on 1 July 2021. He made up his first set of accounts for six months to 31 December 2021 and yearly from then on.

The following fixed asset information is available for his first 18 months of trade:

Date	Additions	Cost £
1 July 21	New plant and machinery.	30,400
15 July 21	A car with CO_2 emissions of 40g/km. Mr Wish used this car 75% of the time for business purposes.	16,000
2 Mar 22	A car with CO_2 emissions of 60g/km. This car is used 20% of the time by a salesman for private purposes.	28,000
2 July 22	A new electric car for Mr Wish with zero emissions. Mr Wish used this car 75% of the time for business purposes.	17,500
13 September 22	New equipment	1,012,000

Date	Disposals	Proceeds £
1 July 22	Mr Wish's car bought on 15 July 21.	15,300

Complete the capital allowance computations for the period ended 31 December 2021 and the year ended 31 December 2022. The brought forward figures of £nil have already been entered.

You should ensure that:

- Any additions qualifying for AIA or FYA are included in the appropriate column
- All allowances are included in the total allowances column
- The total allowances for each period are clearly shown
- Carried forward balances are clearly shown.

Any columns that are not required should be left blank.

	AIA	FYA	General pool	Special rate pool	Private use asset	Total allowances
6 m/e 31/12/21					25%	
TWDV Brought forward			0	0		
Add no FYA, AIA						
Car 40%					16,000	
Car 60g.				28000		
Add FYA						
Car 0g		(17500)				13125
Add AIA						
Equipment	1012,000		12,000			
New Plant	30,400 ?					1,000,000
	(1,000,000)					
Disposal						
			12000	28,000	16,000	
WDA 18% 6/12			(2160)		(1440)(6/12)	3240
WDA 6%				(1680)		1680
Disposal					(15300)	
					(740)	555
c/d			9840	26320	0	
Capital All'w						

75%

2160
1080 75%

Task 3 (6 marks)

This task is about basis period rules.

(a) The following accounts have been prepared for a sole trader: **(4 marks)**

	£
Y/e 30/06/2020	45,000
Y/e 30/06/2021	42,000
Period to 30/11/2021	15,000

The trade ceased on 30 November 2021 and overlap profits from commencement were £9,500.

(i) **The penultimate tax year is: (insert as xxxx/xx)**

(ii) **The final tax year is: (insert as xxxx/xx)**

(iii) **The profits for the penultimate year of trade are:**

£	

(iv) **The profits for the final year of trade are:**

£	

(b) **Identify whether the following statements are true or false.** **(2 marks)**

	True ✓	False ✓
If an individual starts trading on 1 March 2022 their first tax year is 2021/22.		
If an individual chose a 30 April 2022 year end rather than a 31 March 2022 year end the delay by one month in preparing their accounts would actually delay their tax due dates by one year.		

Task 4 (8 marks)

This task is about analysing profits and losses of a partnership and calculating NICs.

(a) Jude and Kelly have been in partnership for many years making up accounts to 30 September each year. They each earn an annual salary of £20,000 and share remaining profits 3:1 respectively.

On 1 July 2021, Liam joined the partnership. It was agreed that Jude and Kelly would continue to earn a salary of £20,000 per year and Liam would be paid a salary of £6,000 per year. Remaining profits would be shared 2:2:1 for Jude, Kelly and Liam.

For the year ended 30 September 2021, the partnership trading profit was £54,000.

Calculate the trading profits for each partner for the year ended 30 September 2021 by completing the missing entries in the appropriation of profits below. All entries should be stated to the nearest pound. **(6 marks)**

	Jude £	Kelly £	Liam £	Total £
Period to 30 June				
Salary			0	AUTOSUM
Profit share			0	
Total	AUTOSUM	AUTOSUM	0	AUTOSUM
Period to 30 September				
Salary				AUTOSUM
Division of profits				
Total	AUTOSUM	AUTOSUM	AUTOSUM	AUTOSUM
Total profit for y/e 30/09/2021	AUTOSUM	AUTOSUM	AUTOSUM	AUTOSUM

(b) Crystal is a sole trader who has been trading for many years, has taxable trading profits of £91,750 for the year ended 31 December 2021.

Crystal's Class 2 NIC liability for 2021/22 is: (show your answer to the nearest penny)

£		.	

Crystal's Class 4 NIC liability for 2021/22 is: (show your answer to the nearest penny)

£		.	

(2 marks)

Task 5 (6 marks)

This task is about chargeable gains and allowable losses for companies.

(a) DEF plc bought a factory for use in its trade on 10 December 2010 for £120,000. It sold the factory for £230,000 on 1 May 2021. **(4 marks)**

Assumed Indexation factors

December 2010 to December 2017 0.218

(i) **Calculate the chargeable gain to be included in the corporation tax computation of DEF plc. Any amounts to be deducted in calculating the gain should be shown as a negative figure (for example, a deduction of 5,000 should be shown as -5000 or -5,000). All entries should be stated to the nearest pound.**

	£
Proceeds	
Cost	
Indexation allowance	
Chargeable gain	AUTOSUM

(ii) If a new factory is acquired for £200,000, the amount of the gain which can be rolled-over is:

£	

(b) Identify whether the following statements are true or false. (2 marks)

	True ✓	False ✓
When a company disposes of an asset any legal fees on disposal are deducted in calculating the gain but legal fees on acquisition are not included.		
Indexation can create but not increase a loss.		

Task 6 (9 marks)

This task is about chargeable gains and allowable losses in company disposal of shares.

In May 2021, Green Ltd sold 4,000 of the shares it held in Blue Ltd for £130,000. These shares had been acquired as follows:

	No. of shares	£
June 1994	4,000	60,000
July 1997 – bonus issue	1 for 10	
September 2002 – rights issue	1 for 5	£10 per share

Indexation factors:

June 1994 to July 1997	0.088
June 1994 to September 2002	0.227
July 1997 to September 2002	0.128
September 2002 to December 2017	0.620

(a)(i) **Complete the share pool for Green Ltd. The purchase in June 1994 has already been included. Show the balance of the shares carried forward. Show your answers to the nearest pound. You have been given more space than you will need.**

	No. of shares	Cost £	Indexed cost £
June 1994 Addition	4,000	60,000	60,000

	No. of shares	Cost £	Indexed cost £

(6 marks)

(ii) Calculate the chargeable gain or allowable loss on the disposal of the shares in Blue Ltd by Green Ltd in May 2021. Show your answers to the nearest pound. You have been given more space than you will need.

(3 marks)

Task 7 (6 marks)

This task is about calculating taxable profits and corporation tax payable.

A company made up accounts to 31 March 2021. It decides to make up its next set of accounts to the 18 months ending 30 September 2022.

(a) **Show how each of the following would be allocated for the long period of account.** (5 marks)

	Amount accrued in period ✓	Time apportioned ✓	Period in which it arose ✓
Trading profits			
Business property income			
Qualifying charitable donation			
Chargeable gains			
Investment income			

(b) **Identify whether the following statement is true or false:** (1 mark)

	True ✓	False ✓
The company would prepare two corporation tax computations. The first for the period to 30 September 2021 and the second for the period to 30 September 2022.		

Task 8 (15 marks)

This task is about administrative requirements of UK tax law.

(a) T Ltd, a large company, has a corporation tax liability of £600,000 in respect of its accounting year ended 31 December 2021.

Identify the date by which the company will be required to pay its FINAL instalment of the liability. Tick ONE box. (1 mark)

	✓
14 October 2021	
14 January 2022	
14 April 2022	
1 October 2022	

(b) More Ltd prepares accounts to 30 September each year. It was given notice by HMRC on 30 November 2021 to file its corporation tax return for the year to 30 September 2021. The return was submitted on 1 December 2022. This was the first late return for the company.

Calculate the maximum penalty payable by More Ltd as a result of its late filing?

£	

(1 mark)

(c) Dayfis Ltd was incorporated on 1 October 2021. The company started to trade on 1 December 2021 and made up its first accounts for the period to 30 June 2022.

Identify the date by which Dayfis Ltd must notify HMRC of its chargeability to corporation tax.

- ○ 1 December 2021
- ○ 1 January 2022
- ○ 1 March 2022
- ○ 30 June 2023

(1 mark)

(d) For the year ended 31 December 2021, Lateness Ltd had a corporation tax liability of £60,000, which it did not pay until 31 March 2023. Lateness Ltd is not a large company.

Identify the number of months of interest Lateness Ltd will be charged by HMRC in respect of the late payment of its corporation tax liability for the year ended 31 December 2021. Show your answer as a number. For example, for the answer two months enter 2 into the box.

(1 mark)

(e) Mina is a self-employed client of yours. She has tax payable for 2021/22 of £4,225, but was not required to make any payments on account for this tax year.

Mina is looking for advice about when she needs to pay this tax. She has also advised you that she accidentally forgot to include quite a substantial trading invoice in her tax return for 2020/21, and is wondering what to do about this and whether she might incur a penalty.

In the box below respond to Mina's query by explaining:

(i) **When she should pay the 2021/22 tax liability** **(1 mark)**

(ii) **How much each payment on account will be for 2022/23 and when these should be paid** **(3 marks)**

(iii) **When the balancing payment 2022/23 would be due and how this is calculated** **(3 marks)**

(iv) **The penalty that she may incur for a careless (non deliberate) error on her return, and what she could do to try and reduce this penalty** **(4 marks)**

Task 9 (12 marks)

This task is about tax planning and the responsibilities of the business and agent.

(a) **Which TWO of the following are not fundamental principles of professional ethics?**

	✓
Confidentiality	
Professional intellect	
Integrity	
Courtesy and consideration	
Professional competence and due care	

(2 marks)

(b) On 8 September 2021 Sylvia purchased a derelict flat for £127,000. She then renovated the house at a cost of £50,000. She completed the renovation on 5 February 2022 and immediately put the house up for sale, and it sold on 1 April 2022 for £200,000. This is the fourth such renovation Sylvia has completed in the last few years.

Sylvia financed the transaction by a bank loan of £150,000 that was taken out on 8 September 2021 at an annual interest rate of 5%. The loan was repaid on 2 April 2022.

Sylvia had no other income or capital gains for the tax year 2021/22 except as indicated above.

Sylvia has been advised that whether or not she is treated as carrying on a trade will be determined according to the 'badges of trade'.

Discuss whether Sylvia is trading by reference to the badges of trade. You should ensure you reach a conclusion. **(6 marks)**

(c) A higher rate tax payer would like to extract profits from their company by way of a dividend. They already receive dividends of £5,000.

Explain the tax consequences of the profit extraction for both the company and the individual.

(3 marks)

(d) **Identify whether the following statement is true or false.**

	True ✓	False ✓
The first £4,000 of employee's NIC is covered by an employment allowance.		

(1 mark)

Task 10 (8 marks)

This task is about trading losses.

(a) **Identify whether the following statements are true or false.** **(4 marks)**

	True ✓	False ✓
A sole trader must make a claim to set a loss made in 2021/22 against total income in 2021/22 before making a claim to set the loss against total income in 2020/21		
A sole trader can carry trade losses forward and choose the best year to use them		
A sole trader can only offset trading losses brought forward against profits of the same trade		
A company can only offset trading losses brought forward against profits of the same trade		

(b) Harley has been trading as a travel consultant for many years earning trade profits of £60,000 each tax year until 2020/21 when he earned trade profits of only £10,000. In 2021/22 he made a trade loss of £80,000 and ceased to trade. He also has £3,000 of property income each tax year.

Explain the loss options available to Harley.

(4 marks)

Task 11 (10 marks)

This task is about business disposals.

Lisa is a higher rate tax payer for income tax purposes. On 31 December 2021 she sells her sole trade business which she set up in 2018. She sells her business for £325,000 with her assets as stated below:

Asset	Market value £	Original cost £	TWDV £
Factory	200,000	115,000	
Plant & machinery	60,000	10,000	10,000
Goodwill	35,000	0	
Inventory	30,000	25,000	

Lisa will pay an additional £23,100 of income tax and national insurance due to the sale of the plant and machinery and inventory.

(a) (i) **Calculate the taxable gain for Lisa on the sale of her business.**

£	

(3 marks)

(ii) Calculate the tax that will be charged on the gain assuming that Lisa claims all beneficial reliefs.

£	

(1 mark)

(iii) Calculate the after-tax proceeds that Lisa will have from the sale of her business.

£	

(3 marks)

(b) Identify the date by which a claim for business asset disposal relief on a disposal in 2021/22 needs to be made.

(1 mark)

(c) Are the following statements true or false?

	True ✓	False ✓
If Lisa had set her business up 1 February 2020, business asset disposal relief would not be available on the disposal.		
If Lisa had gifted the business to her daughter, Lisa alone could have made a claim for gift relief to defer her gain.		

(2 marks)

BPP PRACTICE ASSESSMENT 1
BUSINESS TAX

ANSWERS

Business Tax (BSTX)
BPP practice assessment 1

Task 1

	£
Accounting profit	227,070
Gifts to customers	1,350
New wall	2,200
Irrecoverable debts	400
Motor expenses – George	1,650
Motor expenses – Salesman	0
Wages and salaries	0
Depreciation	21,080
Capital allowances	-15,000
Taxable profit	238,750

Task 2

	AIA	FYA	General pool	Special rate pool	Private use asset	%	Total allowances
6 m/e 31/12/21							
TWDV Brought forward			0	0			
Plant & machinery	30,400						
Mr Wish car					16,000		
AIA	(30,400)						30,400
WDA @ 18% ×6/12					(1,440)	×75%	1,080
Total allowances							31,480
TWDV c/f			0		14,560		
Y/e 31/12/22							
TWDV b/f			0		14,560		
Equipment	1,012,000						

	AIA	FYA	General pool	Special rate pool	Private use asset	%	Total allowances
Salesman car				28,000			
Mr Wish car		17,500					
AIA (max)	(1,000,000)						1,000,000
Transfer to general pool	(12,000)		12,000				
FYA @ 100%		(17,500)				×75%	13,125
Disposal					(15,300)		
					(740)		
Balancing charge					740	×75%	(555)
WDA @ 18%			(2,160)				2,160
WDA @ 6%				(1,680)			1,680
Total allowances							1,016,410
TWDV c/f			9,840	26,320	0		

Task 3

(a) (i) The penultimate tax year is:

2020/21

(ii) The final tax year is:

2021/22

(iii) The profits for the penultimate year of trade are:

£	45,000

(iv) The profits for the final year of trade are:

£	47,500

Working

(£42,000 + £15,000 – £9,500)

(b)

	True ✓	False ✓
If an individual starts trading on 1 March 2022 their first tax year is 2021/22.	✓	
If an individual chose a 30 April 2022 year end rather than a 31 March 2022 year end the delay by one month in preparing their accounts would actually delay their tax due dates by one year.	✓	

Task 4

	Jude £	Kelly £	Liam £	Total £
Period to 30 June				
Salary (£20,000 × 9/12)	15,000	15,000	0	30,000
Profit share (3:1)	7,875	2,625	0	10,500
Total (£54,000 × 9/12)	22,875	17,625	0	40,500
Period to 30 September				
Salary (£20,000 / £6,000 × 3/12)	5,000	5,000	1,500	11,500
Division of profits (2:2:1)	800	800	400	2,000
Total (£54,000 × 3/12)	5,800	5,800	1,900	13,500
Total profit for y/e 30/09/2021	28,675	23,425	1,900	54,000

Crystal's Class 2 NIC liability for 2021/22 is: (show your answer to the nearest penny)

£	158	.	60

Working

(£3.05 × 52)

Crystal's Class 4 NIC liability for 2021/22 is: (show your answer to the nearest penny)

£	4,492	.	78

Working

£(50,270 – 9,568) × 9% + £(91,750 – 50,270) × 2%

= 3,663.18 + 829.60

ANSWERS

Task 5

(a) (i)

	£
Proceeds	230,000
Cost	-120,000
Indexation allowance £120,000 × 0.218	-26,160
Chargeable gain	83,840

(ii) If a new factory is acquired for £200,000, the amount of the gain which can be rolled-over is:

£	53,840

Workings

Gain immediately chargeable £(230,000 – 200,000) = £30,000

Gain which can be rolled-over £(83,840 – 30,000) = £53,840

(b)

	True ✓	False ✓
When a company disposes of an asset any legal fees on disposal are deducted in calculating the gain but legal fees on acquisition are not included. • Both legal fees on acquisition and disposal are included in the gains calculation. Legal fees on disposal are deducted from proceeds to get net proceeds and incidental costs of acquisition are included with the cost figure.		✓
Indexation can create but not increase a loss. • Indexation can never create or increase a loss.		✓

Task 6

(a) (i)

	No. of shares	Cost £	Indexed cost £
June 1994 Addition	4,000	60,000	60,000
July 1997 Bonus issue (N)	400	–	–
	4,400	60,000	60,000
Index to September 2002 0.227 × £60,000			13,620
	4,400	60,000	73,620

	No. of shares	Cost £	Indexed cost £
September 2002 Rights issue	880	8,800	8,800
	5,280	68,800	82,420
Index to December 2017 0.620 × £82,420			51,100
	5,280	68,800	133,520
Less May 2021 Disposal	(4,000)	(52,121)	(101,152)
	1,280	16,679	32,368

Note. There is no need to compute indexation to the date of the bonus issue.

(ii)

Disposal proceeds			130,000
Less cost			(52,121)
Less indexation £(101,152 – 52,121)			(49,031)
Chargeable gain			28,848

Task 7

(a)

	Amount accrued in period ✓	Time apportioned ✓	Period in which it arose ✓
Trading profits		✓	
Business property income	✓		
Qualifying charitable donation			✓
Chargeable gains			✓
Investment income	✓		

(b)

	True ✓	False ✓
The company would prepare two corporation tax computations. The first for the period to 30 September 2021 and the second for the period to 30 September 2022. • The first would be for the 12 m/e 31 March 2022 and the second the 6 m/e 30 September 2022		✓

Task 8

(a)

	✓
14 October 2021	
14 January 2022	
14 April 2022	✓
1 October 2022	

(b) £100

There is a £100 penalty for late return which is submitted within three months of the due date (here 12 months after the end of the period to which the return relates).

(c) 1 March 2022

(d) 6 months

Interest runs from due date (1 October 2022) to the date of payment (31 March 2023) which is six months.

(e)

Task 9

(a)

	✓
Confidentiality	
Professional intellect	✓
Integrity	
Courtesy and consideration	✓
Professional competence and due care	

'Professional intellect' and Courtesy and consideration' would be required of a professional accountant but are not of themselves fundamental principles.

(b) **Length of ownership**

If items purchased are sold soon afterwards, this indicates trading transactions. Sylvia has only owned the house for about seven months which is a short period for ownership of a property and so tends to imply a trade.

Frequency of transactions

Transactions which may, in isolation, be of a capital nature will be interpreted as trading transactions where their frequency indicates the carrying on of a trade. As Sylvia has undertaken four similar renovations in the last two years this would seem to suggest a trade.

Work done

When work is done to make an asset more marketable, or steps are taken to find purchasers, this is likely to be indicative of trading. Sylvia's £50,000 renovation makes it more likely this would be considered trading.

Circumstances of realisation

A forced sale, for example to realise funds for an emergency, is not likely to be treated as trading. Here it appears that Sylvia needs the proceeds to fund her standard of living as she has no other income. This would make it more likely she is considered trading.

Motive

The absence of a profit motive will not necessarily preclude a tax charge as trading income, but its presence is a strong indication that a person is trading. Sylvia appears to have a profit motive in this transaction.

Source of finance

The fact that Sylvia has funded her purchase with a commercial bank loan which she has then immediately repaid following the sale of the flat makes it appear more like a trading transaction.

Conclusion

Taking into account the above badges of trade, it would appear that Sylvia is trading.

(c) The company will pay no national insurance contributions on a dividend. In addition, it will not obtain a corporation tax deduction for the dividend paid.

The individual will pay income tax at 32.5% on the dividend received and no national insurance contributions.

(d)

	True ✓	False ✓
The first £4,000 of employee's NIC is covered by an employment allowance. • The employment allowance is available against employer's not employee's NICs.		✓

Task 10

(a)

	True ✓	False ✓
A sole trader must make a claim to set a loss made in 2021/22 against total income in 2021/22 before making a claim to set the loss against total income in 2020/21 • The CY and/or PY claim can be made in any order		✓
A sole trader can carry trade losses forward and choose the best year to use them • The losses must be offset against the first available profits of the same trade		✓
A sole trader can only offset trading losses brought forward against profits of the same trade	✓	
A company can only offset trading losses brought forward against profits of the same trade • The carry forward of trade losses for a company is against total profits		✓

(b) Harley could make a current year claim to offset his 2021/22 trade loss against his property income of £3,000. This would not save any tax and would waste his personal allowance.

Harley could alternatively make a prior year claim to offset £13,000 of his trade loss against his total income in 2020/21. This would save a small amount of tax at 20% and waste his personal allowance. £67,000 of the trade loss would remain unused.

Alternatively, as Harley has ceased to trade he can make a terminal loss claim to carry back his trade loss three tax years on a last in first out basis against his trade profits only. This would offset £10,000 of trade loss in 2020/21 which would save a small amount of tax at 20% and then waste personal allowance. The remaining £70,000 of trade loss would be carried back and £60,000 could be offset in 2019/20 with the remaining £10,000 in 2018/19. These claims would allow some tax to be saved at 40% in addition to 20% tax savings. It will also give Harley a cashflow advantage of being able to claim a tax refund.

Task 11

(a) (i) £107,700

	£
Gain on factory (£200,000- £115,000)	85,000
Gain on goodwill (£35,000 - £0)	35,000
Less annual exempt amount	(12,300)
Taxable gains	107,700

(ii) £10,770

	£
Taxable gains	107,700
CGT @ 10% (BADR)	10,770

(iii) £291,130

	£
Proceeds	325,000
Less income tax and NIC on adjustment to trade profits (given)	(23,100)
Less capital gains tax on gains @ 10%	(10,770)
After-tax proceeds	291,130

(b) A claim for business asset disposal relief for a disposal made in 2021/22 needs to be made by 31 January 2024.

(c)

	True ✓	False ✓
If Lisa had set her business up 1 February 2020, business asset disposal relief would not be available on the disposal. • Lisa would not have owned the business for the two years required for a BADR claim.	✓	
If Lisa had gifted the business to her daughter, Lisa alone could have made a claim for gift relief to defer her gain. • It is a joint claim rather than a claim that is only made by the donor.		✓

ANSWERS

BPP PRACTICE ASSESSMENT 2
BUSINESS TAX

Time allowed: 2 hours

PRACTICE ASSESSMENT 2

Business Tax (BSTX)
BPP practice assessment 2

In the live assessment you will have access to the Tax tables and reference material which have been reproduced at the back of this Question Bank. Please use them whilst completing this practice assessment so that you are familiar with their content.

Task 1 (8 marks)

This task is about adjusting accounting profits and losses for tax purposes.

The statement of profit or loss for Henry Ltd for the year to 31 December 2022 shows the following information:

	£	£
Gross profit		500,350
Dividends received		4,500
Property business income		7,500
		512,350
General expenses (note 1)	240,780	
Wages and salaries	120,650	
Administrative expenses	87,230	
Depreciation charge	14,600	
		(463,260)
Profit for the year		49,090

Notes.

1 **General expenses**

These include:

	£
Qualifying charitable donation (paid July 2022)	3,500
Entertaining customers	8,450

2 **Capital allowances**

The capital allowances for the year ended 31 December 2022 are £8,750.

(a) **Complete the computation. Do not use minus signs or brackets to show negative figures. Please keep your selected answers in the same order as they appear in the picklist.** **(6 marks)**

Accounting profit	49,090
Add back (Picklist 1)	
▼	
▼	
▼	
Total added back	

Deduct (Picklist 2)	
▼	
▼	
▼	
Taxable profit	

Picklist 1:

Qualifying charitable donation (paid July 2022)
Entertaining customers
Wages and salaries
Administrative expenses
Depreciation charge
Capital allowances

Picklist 2:

Dividends received
Property business income
Administrative expenses
Depreciation charge
Capital allowances

(b) **For each of the following items included in an accounting profit calculation, identify the correct treatment in relation to the computation of the taxable profit.** **(2 marks)**

Staff party £10 per head ▼

Purchase of new motor vehicle ▼

Picklist:

Allowed
Disallowed and add back
Disallowed and deduct

Task 2 (12 marks)

This task is about capital allowances.

(a) Codie Ltd is in business as a sole trader making up accounts to 31 January each year. You have been asked to complete its capital allowances computation for the year to 31 January 2022. The following information is relevant:

(1) The capital allowance computation showed the following written-down values at 1 February 2021:

	£
General pool	58,060
Special rate pool	26,900

(2) During the period 1 February 2021 to 31 January 2022 Codie Ltd had the following capital transactions:

Purchases		£
February 2021	Plant and machinery	100,000
December 2021	Plant and machinery	204,250
January 2022	Car (CO_2 emissions 60g/km) 20% private use of managing director	19,320

Disposals		
January 2022	Zero emission car	23,900

Complete the capital allowance computations for the year ended 31 January 2022. The brought forward figures have already been entered.

You should ensure that:

- Any additions qualifying for AIA, FYA or super deduction are included in the appropriate column
- All allowances are included in the total allowances column
- The total allowances for each period are clearly shown
- Carried forward balances are clearly shown.

Any columns that are not required should be left blank. **(8 marks)**

	AIA	FYA	Super deduction	General pool	Special rate pool	Private use asset	Total allowances
y/e 31/1/22							
TWDV Brought forward				58,060	26,900		

(b) Pear Ltd purchases a newly constructed factory for £1,250,000 including £200,000 for the land and £50,000 in stamp duty and legal fees. The factory was purchased on 1 May 2022 and brought into use in Pear Ltd's trade on 1 June 2022. Pear Ltd has a 31 December year end.

What is the qualifying expenditure in relation to the factory for the structural and buildings allowance? **(2 marks)**

£	

What SBA will Pear Ltd be entitled to in the year ended 31 December 2022? Calculate your answer to the nearest pound. **(1 mark)**

£	

If Pear Ltd were to sell the factory to Banana plc on 31 December 2022 for £1,500,000 (including £200,000 for land and £100,000 in stamp duty and legal fees), on what eligible expenditure would Banana plc claim its structures and buildings allowance? **(1 mark)**

£	

Task 3 (6 marks)

This task is about basis period rules.

Sayed started trading on 1 January 2021. He makes up his accounts to 30 April each year. The profits were calculated as:

	£
Period to 30 April 2021	20,000
Year to 30 April 2022	36,000
Year to 30 April 2023	42,000

Calculate the taxable profits and state the tax year and basis period for the first three tax years of trading. In the basis period column show dates in the format shown, for example 01/01/2021 – 31/07/2021 for 1 January 2021 to 31 July 2021. (6 marks)

Tax year	Basis period DD/MM/YYYY – DD/MM/YYYY	Profit £
2020/21	–	
2021/22	–	
2022/23	–	

Task 4 (8 marks)

This task is about analysing profits and losses of a partnership and calculating NICs.

Xavier, Yvonne and Zebedee have been in partnership for many years making up accounts to 30 September each year. Under the partnership agreement, Xavier was entitled to a salary of £9,000 a year and the profits were then divided 2:2:1 between the partners respectively.

Xavier retired from the partnership on 31 December 2021. Yvonne and Zebedee carried on the partnership and the partnership agreement was altered so that the profits were then divided 2:1 between Yvonne and Zebedee respectively with each being entitled to a £10,000 salary from 1 January 2022.

The partnership profits for the year to 30 September 2022 were £209,000.

(a) **Calculate the trading profits for each partner for the year ended 30 September 2022 by completing the missing entries in the appropriation of profits below. All entries should be stated to the nearest pound.** (6 marks)

	Xavier £	Yvonne £	Zebedee £	Total £
Period to 31/12/2021				
Salary				AUTOSUM
Share of profits				
Total	AUTOSUM	AUTOSUM	AUTOSUM	AUTOSUM

	Xavier £	Yvonne £	Zebedee £	Total £
Period to 30/09/2022				
Salary				AUTOSUM
Share of profits				
Total	AUTOSUM	AUTOSUM	AUTOSUM	AUTOSUM
Total profit for y/e 30/09/2022	AUTOSUM	AUTOSUM	AUTOSUM	AUTOSUM

(b) Jayden starts in business as a sole trader on 6 April 2021. Her adjusted trading profit for the year to 5 April 2022 is £22,500. **(2 marks)**

Jayden's Class 2 NICs payable for 2021/22 are:

£		.	

Jayden's Class 4 NICs payable for 2021/22 are:

£		.	

Task 5 (6 marks)

This task is about chargeable gains and allowable losses for companies.

On 8 September 2021, Daisy plc sold a factory for £900,000. Legal fees of £3,500 were incurred on disposal. The factory had been purchased in April 2000 for £520,000. Legal fees of £2,000 were incurred on acquisition. Daisy plc had spent £40,000 on an extension to the warehouse in August 2018.

Assumed Indexation factors

April 2000 – December 2017 0.635

Calculate the chargeable gain to be included in the corporation tax computation of Daisy plc for the year ended 31 December 2021. Any amounts to be deducted in calculating the gain should be shown as a negative figure (for example, a deduction of 5,000 should be shown as -5,000 or -5000). All entries should be stated to the nearest pound. (6 marks)

	£
Proceeds	
Selling expenses	
Cost including acquisition expenses	
Enhancement expenditure	
Unindexed gain	
Indexation allowance on cost	
Indexation allowance on enhancement	
Chargeable gain	

Task 6 (9 marks)

This task is about chargeable gains and allowable losses in company disposal of shares.

Purple Ltd had the following transactions in the shares of Yellow Ltd:

June 1987	Purchased 1,500 shares for £2,000
May 1989	Purchased 2,500 shares for £6,000
May 2003	Took up one for two rights issue at £3 per share
October 2021	Sold 3,000 shares for £32,000

Assumed Indexation factors

June 1987 to May 1989	0.129
May 1989 to May 2003	0.578
May 2003 to December 2017	0.532

(a) (i) **Complete the share pool for Purple Ltd. The purchase in June 1987 has already been included. Show the balance of the shares carried forward. Show your answers to the nearest pound. You have been given more space than you will need.**

FA85 Share pool

	No. of shares	Cost £	Indexed cost £
June 1987	1,500	2,000	2,000

(6 marks)

(ii) **Calculate the chargeable gain or allowable loss on the disposal of the shares in Yellow Ltd by Purple Ltd in October 2021. Show your answers to the nearest pound.**

	£

(3 marks)

Task 7 (6 marks)

This task is about calculating taxable profits and corporation tax payable.

Carrot plc used to make its accounts up to 31 December. However, the directors decided to change the accounting date to 30 April and make up accounts for a 16-month period to 30 April 2022. The following information relates to the period of account from 1 January 2021 to 30 April 2022:

	£
Adjusted trading profit before capital allowances	500,000
Capital gain on property sold on:	
1 February 2021	16,000
Qualifying charitable donations paid on:	
15 April 2022	10,000

The TWDV of the general pool on 1 January 2021 is £162,000 and there have been no capital purchases or disposals during the 16 month period to 30 April 2022.

Calculate the taxable total profits for each periods by completing the table below. Any amounts decreasing taxable profits should be shown as a negative figure (for example, a deduction of 5,000 should be shown as -5000 or -5,000).

State all answers to the nearest pound. Leave blank any box where no entry is required.

(6 marks)

	First period £	Second period £
Trading profits before capital allowances		
Capital allowances		
Trade profits	AUTOSUM	AUTOSUM
Chargeable gain		
Qualifying charitable donations paid		
Taxable total profits	AUTOSUM	AUTOSUM

Task 8 (15 marks)

This task is about administrative requirements of UK tax law.

(a) (i) **The maximum penalty for failure to keep records for each tax year or accounting period is:**

	✓
£4,000	
£3,000	
£2,500	
£1,500	

(ii) **The maximum penalty for a deliberate but not concealed error as a percentage of Potential Lost Revenue is:**

	✓
70%	
35%	
20%	
15%	

(iii) A taxpayer files his tax return for 2021/22 online on 15 March 2023. His tax liability for the year is £2,000.

The maximum penalty for late filing is:

	✓
£2,000	
£300	
£200	
£100	

(3 marks)

(b) Holly has a liability to capital gains tax in 2021/22.

(i) **She must pay the capital gains tax due by: (insert dates as DD/MM/YYYY)**

Holly is also required to make payments on account for her 2021/22 income tax liability.

(ii) **She must make payments on account of income tax and NIC for 2021/22 by:**

and

(iii) **She must pay the balancing payment by:**

(4 marks)

(c) Petunia Ltd prepared accounts for the year ended 31 March 2022 and has taxable total profits of £171,705, resulting in a corporation tax liability of £32,624.

Petunia Ltd has previously submitted its corporation tax returns on time and had a corporation tax liability for the year to 31 March 2021 of £22,000.

(i) **What is the date by which Petunia Ltd's self-assessment corporation tax return for the year ended 31 March 2022 should be submitted?**

A. 31 December 2022

B. 31 January 2023

C. 31 March 2023

D. 31 July 2023

(1 mark)

(ii) **Calculate the amount of late filing penalties that will be charged on Petunia Ltd if it submits its return and pays the corporation tax due for the year ended 31 March 2022 on 27 November 2023? Show your answers to the nearest pound.**

Penalty	£
Fixed penalty	
Tax-geared penalty	

(2 marks)

(iii) **Identify when Petunia Ltd's corporation tax liability for the year ended 31 March 2022 should have been paid?**

○ £32,624 on 1 January 2023

○ £11,000 on 31 January 2022 and 31 July 2022, £10,624 on 31 January 2023

○ £8,156 on 14 October 2021, 14 January 2022, 14 April 2022 and 14 July 2022

○ £5,500 on 14 October 2021, 14 January 2022 and 14 April 2022, £16,124 on 14 July 2022 **(1 mark)**

(d) **Identify which ONE of the following statements is TRUE?**

○ Individuals with tax payable of less than £1,000 for a tax year are not required to file a self-assessment tax return.

○ Individuals are only required to file a self-assessment tax return for a tax year if they receive a notice to deliver from HM Revenue & Customs (HMRC).

○ Where an online return is filed, a calculation of the liability is made automatically.

○ The self-assessment tax return for an individual covers income tax, class 1, class 2 and class 4 national insurance contributions and capital gains tax liabilities. **(1 mark)**

(e) For the year ended 31 December 2021, Tardy Ltd had a corporation tax liability of £50,000, which it did not pay until 31 March 2023. Tardy Ltd is not a large company.

How many months of interest will Tardy Ltd be charged by HM Revenue & Customs (HMRC) in respect of the late payment of its corporation tax liability for the year ended 31 December 2021? Show your answer as a number. For example, for the answer two months enter 2 into the box.

(1 mark)

QUESTIONS

(f) Pedro is self-employed and also has income from investments.

For each of the types of records listed below, click in the box to indicate the date until which Pedro must retain the records used in preparing his self-assessment tax return for the tax year 2021/22.

Business records	31 JANUARY 2024	31 JANUARY 2028
Non-business records	31 JANUARY 2024	31 JANUARY 2028

(2 marks)

Task 9 (12 marks)

This task is about tax planning and the responsibilities of the business and agent.

(a) **Identify whether the following action by a taxpayer would constitute tax evasion.**

	Tax evasion ✓	Not tax evasion ✓
Earning tax-free dividends in an ISA		

(1 mark)

(b) **Identify which TWO of the following are not badges of trade.**

	Not a badge of trade ✓
The number of transactions	
Provision of own equipment	
Profit seeking motive	
Changes to the asset	
Correction of own work	

(c) Richard is the sole shareholder and director of Ricardo Ltd. The company has several other employees such that the employment allowance is fully utilised.

The company has tax adjusted profits of £23,000 for the year. This is after deducting Richard and his employee's usual salaries and the employer's NICs thereon. Richard would like to take the remaining profits out of the company either by way of a bonus or as a dividend.

Richard has other income of £25,000 which comprises his £20,000 salary from Ricardo Ltd and £5,000 of dividends. He is therefore a basic rate tax payer.

Calculate the after-tax amount received by Richard, if he choses to take the profits as a bonus.

Calculate the after-tax amount received by Richard, if he choses to take the profits as a dividend.

(5 marks)

(d) Simon and Pippa are a married couple. Pippa is a higher rate tax payer and Simon is a basic rate tax payer. Pippa owns some shares which the couple plan to dispose of before the end of the tax year to generate a chargeable gain of £30,000.

Explain how the couple should dispose of the shares to minimise their overall capital gains tax liability.

(4 marks)

Task 10 (8 marks)

This task is about trading losses.

(a) Joe, a sole trader who has been trading for many years, made a trading profit of £4,500 in his year ended 31 January 2021, a trading loss of £65,000 in his year ended 31 January 2022, and he predicts trading profits to be £5,000 for the year ended 31 January 2023. Each tax year he also receives rental income of £19,000.

Joe has a policy of claiming the maximum amount of loss relief as early as possible.

Calculate the amount of trading loss that Joe will relieve against total income in 2020/21?

£	

Calculate the amount of trading loss that Joe will relieve against total income in 2021/22?

£	

Calculate the maximum trading loss that Joe can relieve in 2022/23?

£	

(3 marks)

(b) A limited company makes a trading loss of £47,300 in its year ended 31 March 2022. It has also made a chargeable gain of £52,350 in the same period, and has capital losses brought forward of £5,200. The company has a policy of claiming relief for its losses as soon as possible.

(i) **Calculate the amount of trading loss that can be claimed against profits in the year ended 31 March 2022.**

£	

(ii) **Calculate the amount of trading loss that can be carried forward to the year ended 31 March 2023.**

£	

(3 marks)

(c) **Identify whether the following statements are true or false.**

	True ✓	False ✓
If a sole trader makes a trade loss in their second tax year they can carry back the trade loss three years on a FIFO basis against their trade profits		
When a company ceases to trade it can carry back its trade loss three years on a FIFO basis against trade profits only		
A company must make a current year loss offset before it can carry back a trade loss whereas a sole trader can make current year and/ or prior year loss offsets in any order		

(3 marks)

Task 11 (10 marks)

This task is about business disposals.

(a) Jurgen has run a sole trade business for many years. On 31 January 2022 he retired and gifted his business to his son. Jurgen is a higher rate tax payer and this is his only disposal in 2021/22.

On 31 January 2022 the business assets were value as follows:

Asset	Market value £	Original cost £	TWDV £
Factory	100,000	74,000	
Plant & machinery	10,000	40,000	12,000
Goodwill	40,000	0	
Inventory	1,000	800	

Identify the capital gain or allowable loss that may arise on the disposal of each asset assuming that no reliefs are claimed. If no gain or loss arises, enter 0. Any loss should be shown as a negative number. **(4 marks)**

Asset	Capital gain/(loss)
Factory	
Plant & machinery	
Goodwill	
Inventory	

(b) **Identify whether each of the following statements is true or false:**

Statement	True ✓	False ✓
A gift relief claim will need to be made by Jurgen alone.		
Jurgen needs to have run the business for two years before the gift relief claim is available.		
The effect of the gift relief claim is to give Jurgen's son a larger gain on his future disposal of the chargeable assets.		

(3 marks)

(c) Chris has owned 100% of the shares in Primrose Ltd, an unquoted trading company, for the last three years. He makes a chargeable gain of £1,100,000 on disposal of the shares.

Identify one other condition that must be satisfied in order for the disposal to qualify for business asset disposal relief. **(1 mark)**

Calculate the CGT due on Chris's disposal, assuming business asset disposal relief is available.

(2 marks)

BPP PRACTICE ASSESSMENT 2 BUSINESS TAX

ANSWERS

Business Tax (BSTX)
BPP practice assessment 2

Task 1

(a)

Accounting profit	49,090
Add back	
Qualifying charitable donation (paid July 2022)	3,500
Entertaining customers	8,450
Depreciation charge	14,600
Total added back	26,550
Deduct	
Dividends received	4,500
Property business income	7,500
Capital allowances	8,750
Taxable profit	54,890

(b) Staff party £10 per head: Allowed

Purchase of new motor vehicle: Disallowed and add back

Task 2

(a)

	AIA	FYA	Super deduction	General pool	Special rate pool	Private use asset	Total allowances
y/e 31/1/22							
TWDV Brought forward				58,060	26,900		
Additions							
Feb 21 P&M	100,000						
Dec 21 P&M			204,250				
Jan 22 Car					19,320		
AIA	(100,000)						100,000
Super deduction (130%)			(204,250)				265,525

	AIA	FYA	Super deduction	General pool	Special rate pool	Private use asset	Total allowances
Disposal				(23,900)			
				34,160	46,220		
WDA @ 18%				(6,149)			6,149
WDA @ 6%					(2,773)		2,773
Total allowances							374,447
TWDV c/f				28,011	43,447		

(b) The qualifying expenditure is £1,000,000. Land, stamp duty and legal fees do not qualify.

The SBA for Pear Ltd for the y/e 31/12/22 = £1,000,000 × 3% × 7/12

= £17,500

Banana plc will be able to claim its SBA based on £1,000,000. The increase in value of the building does not impact the qualifying cost of the building.

Task 3

Tax year	Basis period XX/XX/XXXX – XX/XX/XXXX	Profit £
2020/21	01/01/2021 – 05/04/2021	15,000
2021/22	01/01/2021 – 31/12/2021	44,000
2022/23	01/05/2021 – 30/04/2022	36,000

Working

Second year: Period ending 30 April 2021 plus 8 months to 31 December 2021

£20,000 + (8/12 × £36,000) = £44,000

Task 4

(a)

	Xavier £	Yvonne £	Zebedee £	Total £
Period to 31/12/2021				
Salary (× 3/12)	2,250	0	0	2,250
Share of profits (2:2:1)	20,000	20,000	10,000	50,000
Total	22,250	20,000	10,000	52,250
Period to 30/09/2022				
Salary	0	7,500	7,500	15,000

	Xavier £	Yvonne £	Zebedee £	Total £
Share of profits (2:1)	0	94,500	47,250	141,750
Total	0	102,000	54,750	156,750
Total profit for y/e 30/09/2022	22,250	122,000	64,750	209,000

(b) Jayden's Class 2 NICs payable for 2021/22 are:

£	158	.	60

Working

(£3.05 × 52)

Jayden's Class 4 NICs payable for 2021/22 are:

£	1,163	.	88

Working

(22,500 – 9,568) × 9%.

Task 5

	£
Proceeds	900,000
Selling expenses	-3,500
Cost including acquisition expenses	-522,000
Enhancement expenditure	-40,000
Unindexed gain	334,500
Indexation allowance on cost 0.635 × £522,000	-331,470
Indexation allowance on enhancement	0
Chargeable gain	3,030

ANSWERS

Task 6

(a) (i) FA85 Share pool

	No. of shares	Cost £	Indexed cost £
June 1987	1,500	2,000	2,000
Indexed rise to May 1989			
£2,000 × 0.129			258
			2,258
May 1989	2,500	6,000	6,000
	4,000	8,000	8,258
Indexed rise to May 2003			
£8,258 × 0.578			4,773
			13,031
Rights issue 1:2 @ £3	2,000	6,000	6,000
	6,000	14,000	19,031
Indexed rise to December 2017			
£19,031 × 0.532			10,124
	6,000	14,000	29,155
October 2021 Disposal	(3,000)	(7,000)	(14,578)
Pool c/f	3,000	7,000	14,577

(ii)

	£
Disposal proceeds	32,000
Less cost	(7,000)
	25,000
Less indexation (£14,578 – £7,000)	(7,578)
Chargeable gain	17,422

Task 7

	First period £	Second period £
Trading profits before capital allowances £500,000 × 12/16 : 4/16	375,000	125,000
Capital allowances £162,000 × 18% = £29,160 (£162,000 - £29,160) × 18% x 4/12= £7,970	-29,160	-7,970
Trade profits	345,840	117,030
Chargeable gain	16,000	
Qualifying charitable donations paid		-10,000
Taxable total profits	361,840	107,030

Task 8

(a) (i)

	✓
£4,000	
£3,000	✓
£2,500	
£1,500	

(ii)

	✓
70%	✓
35%	
20%	
15%	

(iii)

	✓
£2,000	
£300	
£200	
£100	✓

Initial penalty for filing return late is £100. As it is less than 3 months late no further penalty is payable.

ANSWERS

(b) (i) She must pay the capital gains tax due by:

31/01/2023

(ii) She must make payments on account **of income tax and NIC** for 2021/22 by:

31/01/2022

and

31/07/2022

(iii) She must pay the balancing payment by:

31/01/2023

(c) (i) C. 31 March 2023

The CT return must be submitted by one year after the end of the period of account ie by 31 March 2023.

(ii)

Penalty	£
Fixed penalty	**200**
Tax-geared penalty	**3,262**

As the return is more than three months late the fixed penalty is £200. As the return is more than six months late there is also a tax geared penalty of 10% × unpaid tax, ie £32,624 × 10% = £3,262. The total amount of penalties is therefore £(200 + 3,262) = £3,462.

(iii) £32,624 on 1 January 2023

As the company is not large since its profits are below the profit threshold of £1,500,000 it must pay its corporation tax by nine months and one day after the accounting period, ie by 1 January 2023.

(d) Where an online return is filed, a calculation of the liability is made automatically.

(e) Interest runs from due date (1 October 2022) to the date of payment (31 March 2023) which is six months.

(f)

Business records		**31 JANUARY 2028**
Non-business records		**31 JANUARY 2028**

Records must be retained until five years after the 31 January following the tax year where the taxpayer is in business. This applies to all of Pedro's records, not just the business records.

Task 9

(a)

	Tax evasion	Not tax evasion
Earning tax-free dividends in an ISA		✓

Earning tax free dividends in an ISA is a legitimate way to reduce tax.

(b)

	Not a badge of trade ✓
The number of transactions	
Provision of own equipment	✓
Profit seeking motive	
Changes to the asset	
Correction of own work	✓

(c) If Richard choses to take the profits as a bonus, he will receive £13,744 after-tax.

	£
Ricardo Ltd's TTP	23,000
Employer's NIC will be due at 13.8% on any salary that Richard chooses to take from the company. So, the TTP figures represents 113.8% of the salary. Employer's NIC on salary to withdraw (13.8/113.8 × £23,000) (Note)	(2,789)
Salary for Richard to withdraw (100/113.8 × £23,000)	20,211
This salary will be taxed on Richard, a basic rate taxpayer, at a rate of 20% income tax and 12% employee's NICs. Thus 32% tax will be suffered (32% × £20,211)	(6,467)
After tax salary kept by Richard	13,744

Note. the employment allowance has already been used and so is not available here.

If Richard choses to take the profits as a dividend, he will receive £17,233 after-tax.

	£
Ricardo Ltd's TTP	23,000
Less corporation tax @ 19%	(4,370)
Profits available to distribute as a dividend = dividend	18,630
As a basic rate taxpayer, Richard will suffer 7.5% income tax on this dividend with no NIC. (7.5% × £18,630)	(1,397)
After-tax dividend kept by Richard	17,233

(d) If Pippa sells the shares and generates the £30,000 chargeable gain the first £12,300 will be covered by her annual exempt amount and then the excess will be taxed at 20% as she is a higher rate tax payer.

The couple's CGT liability would be reduced if they could utilise both Simon and Pippa's annual exempt amounts and then tax any remaining gain on Simon rather than Pippa to access the 10% CGT rate that he is entitled to as a basic rate tax payer.

The couple should therefore pass sufficient shares from Pippa to Simon to leave Pippa generating a £12,300 gain. The transfer of the shares from Pippa to Simon will take place at nil gain nil loss for capital gains tax purposes and the remaining gain is taxable on Simon after applying his annual exempt amount.

Task 10

(a) The trading loss which Joe will relieve against total income in 2020/21 is:

£	23,500

(£4,500 + £19,000) The loss cannot be restricted to save the personal allowance

The trading loss which Joe will relieve against total income in 2021/22 is:

£	19,000

The loss cannot be restricted to save the personal allowance

The maximum trading loss Joe can relieve in 2022/23 is:

£	5,000

Losses can only be offset against trading profits when carried forward.

(b) (i) The amount of trading loss that can be claimed against profits in year ended 31 March 2022 is:

£	47,150

Working

(£52,350 – £5,200)

(ii) The amount of trading loss that can be carried forward to the year ended 31 March 2023 is:

£	150

(c)

	True ✓	False ✓
If a sole trader makes a trade loss in their second tax year they can carry back the trade loss three years on a FIFO basis against their trade profits • The carry back is against total income not trade profits		✓
When a company ceases to trade it can carry back its trade loss three years on a FIFO basis against trade profits only • The carry back is LIFO not FIFO and is against total profits if a loss of the last 12 months		✓

	True ✓	False ✓
A company must make a current year loss offset before it can carry back a trade loss whereas a sole trader can make current year and/ or prior year loss offsets in any order	✓	

Task 11

(a)

Asset	Capital gain/(loss)
Factory	26,000
Plant & machinery	0
Goodwill	40,000
Inventory	0

(b)

Statement	True ✓	False ✓
A gift relief claim will need to be made by Jurgen alone. • A joint claim is required.		✓
Jurgen needs to have run the business for two years before the gift relief claim is available. • There is no time requirement for gift relief		✓
The effect of the gift relief claim is to give Jurgen's son a larger gain on his future disposal of the chargeable assets.	✓	

(c) In order for the disposal to qualify for business asset disposal relief, Chris needs to be employed by Primrose Ltd (and have been employed for at least two years).

Chargeable gain	£1,100,000
AEA	(£12,300)
Taxable gain	£1,087,700
CGT	
£1,000,000 @ 10%	£100,000
£87,700 @ 20%	£17,540
Total CGT	£117,540

ANSWERS

BPP PRACTICE ASSESSMENT 3
BUSINESS TAX

Time allowed: 2 hours

PRACTICE ASSESSMENT 3

Business Tax (BSTX)
BPP practice assessment 3

In the live assessment you will have access to the Tax tables and reference material which have been reproduced at the back of this Question Bank. Please use them whilst completing this practice assessment so that you are familiar with their content.

Task 1 (8 marks)

This task is about adjusting accounting profits and losses for tax purposes.

The statement of profit or loss Jeremy Ltd for the year to 31 March 2022 shows the following information:

	£	£
Gross profit		512,500
Profit on sale of shares		13,550
Dividends received		6,300
Interest income		4,500
		536,850
General expenses (note 1)	210,780	
Wages and salaries	110,350	
		(321,130)
Profit for the year		215,720

Notes.

1 **General expenses**

These include:

	£
Qualifying charitable donation (paid August 2021)	500
Legal fees on renewal of a 70-year lease on the factory	9,550
Replacement of single glazed windows with double glazed windows in the offices	8,650
Redecoration of offices	2,300

Calculate the taxable trading profit for for Jeremy Ltd for the year to 31 March 2022. Fill in all unshaded boxes. Add a 0 (zero) if necessary. Do not use minus signs or brackets for figures in the deduct column. **(8 marks)**

	£	£
Accounting profit		215,720
	Add	Deduct
Profit on sale of shares		
Dividends received		
Interest income		

	£	£
Qualifying charitable donation		
Legal fees on lease renewal		
Replacement windows		
Redecoration of offices		
Wages and salaries		
Total to add/deduct	AUTOSUM	AUTOSUM
Taxable profit		AUTOSUM

Task 2 (12 marks)

This task is about capital allowances.

(a) Ian Goodwin commenced trading on 1 October 2021, and made his first accounts up to 31 March 2022. Ian Goodwin's capital transactions from the date of commencement are:

Additions:		£
1 October 2021	Plant and machinery	310,000
1 December 2021	Motor van	35,500
1 February 2022	Car, 30% private usage by Ian (CO_2 emissions 52g/km)	9,600
15 March 2022	Car, 20% private usage by an employee (zero CO_2 emissions)	12,500
20 March 2022	Car, 10% private usage by an employee (CO_2 emissions 42g/km)	45,500

Complete the capital allowance computations for the period ended 31 March 2022. The brought forward figures of £nil have already been entered.

You should ensure that:

- **Any additions qualifying for AIA or FYA are included in the appropriate column**
- **All allowances are included in the total allowances column**
- **The total allowances for each period are clearly shown**
- **Carried forward balances are clearly shown.**

Any columns that are not required should be left blank. **(8 marks)**

	AIA	FYA	General pool	Special rate pool	Private use asset	Total allowances
6 m/e 31/3/22						
TWDV Brought forward			0	0		

	AIA	FYA	General pool	Special rate pool	Private use asset	Total allowances

(b) **Identify whether the following statements are true or false.** (4 marks)

	True ✓	False ✓
In calculating capital allowances for a 6-month period the WDA, FYA and AIA are all time apportioned.		
When a business ceases to trade, no AIAs or FYAs are given. However, additions and disposals are included and WDAs are then given.		
A super deduction of 130% is available on all purchases made by a company.		
When calculating the SBA available on disposal of an SBA asset the calculation is time apportioned based on when the asset is sold.		

Task 3 (6 marks)

This task is about basis period rules.

(a) If a sole trader has an annual accounting date of 31 December, the profits of the year ended 31 December 2021 will be taxed in which tax year? (insert as XXXX/XX)

For a sole trader with a 30 September year end date, which set of accounts would be taxed in 2021/22? (insert as XX/XX/XXXX)

Y/e

(2 marks)

(b) **Identify whether the following statements are true or false.**

	True ✓	False ✓
If a trader ceases trading on 1 December 2021 their final tax year will be 2020/21.		
If overlap profits were incurred on commencement of trade these reduce the size of a loss (if one is incurred) in the final period.		
Every £ of profit over the life of a sole trade business is only taxed once.		
A 30 April period end date maximises overlap profits.		

(4 marks)

Task 4 (8 marks)

This task is about analysing profits and losses of a partnership and calculating NICs.

(a) Harry, Millie and Richard have been in partnership for many years making up accounts to 30 June each year. They each earn an interest on capital at 5% on their capital invested of £20,000; £20,000 and £60,000 respectively. Any remaining profits are shared equally.

On 1 January 2021, the partnership agreement was altered. The residual profit share was amended to 2:2:3 respectively.

For the year ended 30 June 2021, the partnership trading profit was £89,000.

Calculate the trading profits for each partner for the year ended 30 June 2021 by completing the missing entries in the appropriation of profits below. All entries should be stated to the nearest pound.. Fill in all unshaded boxes and add a 0 (zero) if necessary. (6 marks)

	Harry £	Millie £	Richard £	Total £
Period to 31 December				
Interest on capital			0	AUTOSUM
Profit share			0	
Total	AUTOSUM	AUTOSUM	0	AUTOSUM
Period to 30 June				
Interest on capital				AUTOSUM
Profit share				
Total	AUTOSUM	AUTOSUM	AUTOSUM	AUTOSUM
Total profit for y/e 30/06/21	AUTOSUM	AUTOSUM	AUTOSUM	AUTOSUM

(b) Alan has trade profits of £6,000 for 2021/22. Brian has trade profits of £52,000 for 2021/22. (2 marks)

Alan's Class 4 NICs payable for 2021/22 are:

£		.	

Brian's Class 4 NICs payable for 2021/22 are:

£		.	

Task 5 (6 marks)

This task is about chargeable gains and allowable losses for companies.

On 1 August 2020 Daffodil Ltd sold a factory (old factory) for £800,000 realising a gain of £321,400. Daffodil Ltd replaced the factory with a smaller property (new factory) acquired on 31 March 2022. This property cost £740,000.

(a) **Calculate the gain chargeable on Daffodil Ltd if a claim for rollover relief is made.**

£	

(1 mark)

(b) **Calculate the amount of rollover relief claimed.**

£	

(1 mark)

(c) **Calculate the base cost of the new factory.**

£	

(1 mark)

(d) **Identify whether the following statements are true or false.**

(3 marks)

	True ✓	False ✓
If Daffodil Ltd had reinvested in a larger new factory for £900,000 in July 2019, the full gain could have been deferred.		
If Daffodil Ltd had **also** reinvested in a small warehouse for £100,000 in September 2022, the full gain could have been deferred.		
The effect of the rollover relief claim is that there will be a larger gain when the new factory is sold in the future.		

Task 6 (9 marks)

This task is about chargeable gains and allowable losses in company disposal of shares.

Treasure Ltd sold 2,500 shares in Williams Ltd for £102,100 in June 2021.

2,000 shares had been bought in November 2001 for £50,000.

In June 2003 there was a 1 for 4 bonus issue, when the market value of the shares was £10 per share.

In February 2006, Treasure Ltd took up a rights issue of 1 for 5 shares, at £40 per share.

Indexation factors

November 2001 to June 2003	0.044
June 2003 to February 2006	0.071
November 2001 to February 2006	0.119
February 2006 to December 2017	0.432

(a) (i) Complete the share pool for Green Ltd. The purchase in June 1994 has already been included. Show the balance of the shares carried forward. Show your answers to the nearest pound. You have been given more space than you will need. **(6 marks)**

	No. of shares	Cost £	Indexed cost £
November 2001	2,000	50,000	50,000

	No. of shares	Cost £	Indexed cost £

(ii) **Calculate the chargeable gain or allowable loss on the disposal of the Williams Ltd shares by Treasure Ltd in June 2021. Show your answer to the nearest pound.** **(3 marks)**

	£

Task 7 (6 marks)

This task is about calculating taxable profits and corporation tax payable.

(a) In the year ended 31 March 2022, Brocolli Ltd had taxable trading profits before capital allowances of £1,325,600. In January 2022 Brocolli Ltd sold an asset for £500,000 resulting in a chargeable gain of £100,000. An accounting profit on disposal of the asset of £50,000 had been charged in Broccoli Ltd's financial statements. During the year Brocolli Ltd accrued interest income of £23,000 and paid £12,000 to charity. Capital allowances for the year ended 31 March 2022 have been calculated as £365,200.

Calculate the taxable total profits ans tax liability of Brocolli Ltd's for the year ended 31 March 2022 by completing the table below. Any amounts decreasing taxable profits should be shown with a negative figure (for example, a deduction of 5,000 should be shown as -5000 or -5,000). State all answers to the nearest pound. **(5 marks)**

	£
Trading profits after capital allowances	
Investment income	
Chargeable gain	

	£
Qualifying charitable donations	
Taxable total profit	AUTOSUM
Corporation tax liability	

(b) Identify whether the following statement is true or false: **(1 mark)**

	True ✓	False ✓
Interest payable on a loan to invest in plant and machinery is deductible in calculating a trading company's investment income.		

QUESTIONS

Task 8 (15 marks)

This task is about administrative requirements of UK tax law.

(a) You have been instructed by a new client who started trading on 1 May 2021. He is concerned about some important dates when he should contact HMRC. He has never been required to file a tax return.

Identify, by inserting dates in the format DD/MM/YYYY,

(i) **The date by which he should inform HM Revenue & Customs that he is chargeable to income tax:** **(1 mark)**

(ii) **The date by which his first tax return should be filed, if it is to be filed online:** **(1 mark)**

(iii) **The date by which income tax will have to be paid (assuming he has any) for his first tax year of trading:** **(1 mark)**

(iv) **The date until which he must keep his business records in relation to his first tax year as a trader:** **(1 mark)**

(v) **The date of his first payment on account in respect of his income tax and Class 4 national insurance for his second tax year as a trader:** **(1 mark)**

(b) SR plc makes up accounts to 31 October each year. It is not a large company.

The corporation tax liability of SR plc for the year to 31 October 2021 was £24,000 and for the year to 31 October 2022 was £36,000.

(i) **Identify the correct method for SR plc to pay the corporation tax liability for the year to 31 October 2022? (1 mark)**

	✓
Four instalments of £6,000 each due on 14 May 2022, 14 August 2022, 14 November 2022 and 14 February 2023 with a balancing payment of £12,000 due on 14 April 2023	
One payment due on 31 January 2024	
Four instalments of £9,000 each due on 14 May 2022, 14 August 2022, 14 November 2022 and 14 February 2023	
One payment due on 1 August 2023	

(ii) **Identify whether the following statements are true or false. (3 marks)**

	True ✓	False ✓
The maximum penalty for an error in a tax return which is deliberate but not concealed is 75%.		
If an individual files their 2021/22 tax return online on 13 January 2023, HMRC can start an enquiry at any time before 31 January 2024.		
If a company files its tax return two months late, the penalty is £100.		

(c) Melton plc prepared accounts for the 12-month period to 31 July 2021. There will not be a compliance check into this accounting period.

Complete the sentence below by selecting from the picklist.

Melton plc will be liable for a penalty of up to [▼] if it does not retain its records until [▼].

Date of retention

Picklist:

31 July 2023
31 July 2027

Maximum penalty

Picklist:

£1.000
£3,000

(2 marks)

(d) Charlotte's tax payable for the tax years 2020/21 and 2021/22 is as follows:

	2020/21	*2021/22*
	£	£
Income tax on trading income	9,000	10,600
Class 2 NIC	159	159
Class 4 NIC	1,350	1,800
Capital gains tax	1,750	4,970

Charlotte made the appropriate payments on account on 31 January 2022 and 31 July 2022.

Calculate the amount payable by 31 January 2023 in respect of the tax year 2021/22.

- ○ £2,050
- ○ £7,179
- ○ £7,020
- ○ £5,270

(1 marks)

(e) **Complete the sentence below by selecting from the picklist.**

A sole trader is required to keep their accounting records for [▼] months after the [▼]

Number of months	**Period**
Picklist:	**Picklist:**
12	End of the tax year
60	31 January that follows the end of the tax year

(2 marks)

(f) Tulip plc accidentally recorded its property income incorrectly in its corporation tax return for the year ended 31 March 2021. It reported the mistake to HMRC as soon as this was noticed.

Identify the minimum % penalty which could be levied on Tulip plc for this error.

[ ] %

(1 mark)

Task 9 (12 marks)

This task is about tax planning and the responsibilities of the business and agent.

(a) Frank is considering setting up his own business. He expects to make profits of £100,000 a year for the first few years. He isn't sure whether to set his business up as a sole trader or a company.

If he sets up as a sole trade business he plans to extract £50,000 each year as drawings. If he sets up as a company he will take a £50,000 each year as a salary.

(i) **Explain the tax implications of each business structure Frank is considering, identifying which types of tax will be due and at what rates. You are not required to complete tax computations.** **(5 marks)**

(ii) Discuss whether it would be preferable for Frank and the company, for him to take a lower salary and instead extract profits by way of a dividend, if he sets up the business as a company. (4 marks)

(b) Your firm of accountants acts for Jim. When completing Jim's self-assessment tax return for 2021/22, you discover that Jim gave 100 shares in Sunflower Ltd to his daughter. You have explained to him that this gives rise to a large capital gains tax liability, because the proceeds will be deemed to be the market value at the date of the gift. Instead, Jim has suggested using a figure for proceeds which is much lower than he knows the market value to be on all official documentation to improve the position of the transfer. Jim considers this to be appropriate tax planning.

Explain whether Jim is engaged in tax avoidance, tax planning or tax evasion and the possible implications for Jim if it is considered to be tax evasion. (3 marks)

Task 10 (8 marks)

This task is about trading losses.

(a) Zowie Ltd, a trading company, made a trading loss of £100,000 in its year ended 31 March 2022. It has trading income of £500,000 in each of the years ending 31 March 2021 and 2023, and other income of £250,000 in each of the years ending 31 March 2021, 2022 and 2023.

Identify whether the following statements are true or false. (3 marks)

	True ✓	False ✓
Zowie Ltd can set its loss against its total income in the year ended 31 March 2021.		
Zowie Ltd can set its loss against its total income in the year ended 31 March 2022.		
Zowie Ltd can set its loss against its total income in in the year ended 31 March 2023.		

(b) Donna has traded for many years, making up accounts to 30 June each year. Her recent results have been:

Year ended	£
30 June 2020	32,000
30 June 2021	(66,000)
30 June 2022	18,000

She received property income as follows:

	£
2020/21	6,000
2021/22	16,000
2022/23 (estimate)	21,000

Using the proforma layout provided, calculate Donna's net income for 2020/21 to 2022/23, assuming maximum claims for loss relief are made as early as possible. If no entry is required in a box enter a zero. Show the offset of losses within brackets. For example relieving a loss of 5,000 should be shown as (5000) or (5,000). Fill in all boxes. (5 marks)

	2020/21 £	2021/22 £	2022/23 £
Trading profits			
Trading loss offset against future year			
Property income			
Trading loss offset against current year			
Trading loss offset against previous year			
Net income			

Task 11 (10 marks)

This task is about business disposals.

(a) Giovanni sells his sole trade business at market value. He has made trading profits of £40,000 in his final period and has £1,000 of overlap profits.

Identify the impact that a disposal of each of the assets described below will have on trading profits by dragging the appropriate response into the 'impact' column. Each response can be used more than once.

Asset	Market value £	Original cost £	TWDV £	Impact
Factory	323,000	300,000		
Warehouse	110,000	100,000		
Plant & machinery	10,000	70,000	5,000	
Goodwill	40,000	0		
Inventory	15,000	17,000		

Drag and drop options:

Chargeable gain
Capital loss
Increase in trading profit
Decrease in trading profit

(5 marks)

(b) Isabella is disposing of shares in Willis Ltd on 31 December 2021. On the same day her friend Sam is disposing of his 20% shareholding in the family manufacturing company, Turrell Ltd that he has been a director of for 10 years.

Identify whether each of the following statements are true or false.

Statement	True ✓	False ✓
If Isabella, who owned 100% of the shares in Willis Ltd, had worked for the company and owned the shares for 10 years and Willis Ltd is an investment company, she will qualify for business asset disposal relief giving her a 10% tax rate on her gains.		
If Turrell Ltd had ceased to trade on 31 December 2020, the disposal of shares in December 2021 will not qualify for business asset disposal relief.		

(2 marks)

(c) Frederico disposes of his 100% shareholding in Rosemary Ltd, an unquoted trading company, for £600,000. He had worked for Rosemary Ltd since he set the company up in 2000 when he had acquired his shares for £100,000.

Calculate Frederico's after-tax proceeds on disposal of the Rosemary Ltd shares.

(3 marks)

QUESTIONS

BPP PRACTICE ASSESSMENT 3 BUSINESS TAX

ANSWERS

Business Tax (BSTX)
BPP practice assessment 3

Task 1

Jeremy Ltd adjusted trading profit for the year ending 31 March 2022

	£	£
Accounting profit		215,720
	Add	Deduct
Profit on sale of shares	0	13,550
Dividends received	0	6,300
Interest income	0	4,500
Qualifying charitable donation	500	0
Legal fees on lease renewal	9,550	0
Replacement windows	0	0
Redecoration of offices	0	0
Wages and salaries	0	0
Total to add/deduct	10,050	24,350
Taxable profit		201,420

Task 2

(a)

	AIA	FYA	General pool	Special rate pool	Private use asset	%	Total allowances
6 m/e 31/3/22							
TWDV Brought forward			0				
Plant and machinery	310,000						
Motor van	35,500						
Ian's car					9,600		
Employee car 1		12,500					
Employee car 2			45,500				
AIA (Note)	(345,500)						345,500
FYA @ 100%		(12,500)					12,500

ANSWERS

	AIA	FYA	General pool	Special rate pool	Private use asset	%	Total allowances
WDA @ 18% × 6/12			(4,095)				4,095
WDA @ 6% × 6/12					(288)	× 70%	202
Total allowances							362,297
TWDV c/f			41,105		9,312		

(b)

	True ✓	False ✓
In calculating capital allowances for a 6-month period the WDA, FYA and AIA are all time apportioned. • The WDA and AIA limit are time apportioned for the length of the accounting period but the FYA is never time apportioned.		✓
When a business ceases to trade, no AIAs or FYAs are given. However, additions and disposals are included and WDAs are then given. • In the period trade ceases no AIA, FYA or WDAs are given.		✓
A super deduction of 130% is available on all purchases made by a company. • The super deduction is only available on new main pool plant and machinery (excluding cars.) In addition, it is only available on purchases after 1 April 2021.		✓
When calculating the SBA available on disposal of an SBA asset the calculation is time apportioned based on when the asset is sold.	✓	

Task 3

(a)

2021/22

Y/e 30/09/2021

(b)

	True ✓	False ✓
If a trader ceases trading on 1 December 2021 their final tax year will be 2020/21. • 2021/22 is the final tax year.		✓

	True ✓	False ✓
If overlap profits were incurred on commencement of trade these reduce the size of a loss (if one is incurred) in the final period. • Overlap profits would increase the size of a loss (they decrease the taxable profits)		✓
Every £ of profit over the life of a sole trade business is only taxed once.	✓	
A 30 April period end date maximises overlap profits.	✓	

Task 4

(a)

	Harry £	Millie £	Richard £	Total £
Period to 31 December				
Interest on capital 5% × 6/12 × £20,000/£20,000/£60,000	500	500	1,500	2,500
Profit share (1:1:1)	14,000	14,000	14,000	42,000
Total	14,500	14,500	15,500	44,500
Period to 30 June				
Interest on capital 5% × 6/12 × £20,000/£20,000/£60,000	500	500	1,500	2,500
Profit share (2:2:3)	12,000	12,000	18,000	42,000
Total	12,500	12,500	19,500	44,500
Total profit for y/e 30/06/21	27,000	27,000	35,000	89,000

(b) **Alan's Class 4 NICs payable for 2021/22 are:**

£	0	.	00

Alan's trade profits are below £9,568 such that no Class 4 NIC (nor Class 2 NICs) will be due.

Brian's Class 4 NICs payable for 2021/22 are:

£	3,697	.	78

(£50,270 - £9,568) × 9% + (£52,000 - £50,270) × 2% = £3,697.78

Task 5

(a) The gain chargeable is the proceeds not reinvested = £800,000 - £740,000 = £60,000
(b) The rollover relief claimed = £321,400 - £60,000 = £261,400
(c) The base cost of the new factory = £740,000 - £261,400 = £478,600
(d)

	True ✓	False ✓
If Daffodil Ltd had reinvested in a larger new factory for £900,000 in July 2019, the full gain could have been deferred. • The reinvestment would need to take place in the one year before the disposal of the old factory.		✓
If Daffodil Ltd had **also** reinvested in a small warehouse for £100,000 in September 2022, the full gain could have been deferred.	✓	
The effect of the rollover relief claim is that there will be a larger gain when the new factory is sold in the future.	✓	

Task 6

Share pool

	No. of shares	Cost £	Indexed cost £
November 2001	2,000	50,000	50,000
Bonus issue 1 for 4	500		
	2,500	50,000	50,000
Index to February 2006			
£50,000 × 0.119			5,950
Rights issue 1 for 5 @ £40 each	500	20,000	20,000
	3,000	70,000	75,950
Index to December 2017			
£75,950 × 0.432			32,810
	3,000	70,000	108,760
Less sale	(2,500)	(58,333)	(90,633)
Carry forward	500	11,667	18,127

Gain

			£
Disposal proceeds			102,100
Less cost			(58,333)
			43,767
Indexation (90,633 – 58,333)			(32,300)
Chargeable gain			11,467

Task 7

(a)

	£
Trading profits after capital allowances (£1,325,600 - £365,200)	960,400
Investment income	23,000
Chargeable gain	100,000
Qualifying charitable donations	-12,000
Taxable total profit	1,071,400
Corporation tax liability	203,566

(b)

	True ✓	False ✓
Interest payable on a loan to invest in plant and machinery is deductible in calculating a trading company's investment income. • Interest on a loan to purchase plant and machinery is a trade interest expense and is deductible in calculating the trading profits on which a company is taxed. Non-trading interest expenses are deducted in calculating investment income.		✓

Task 8

(a) (i) The date when he should inform HM Revenue & Customs that he is chargeable to income tax:

05/10/2022

(ii) The date when his first tax return should be filed, if it is to be filed online:

31/01/2023

(iii) The date income tax will need to be paid (assuming he has any) for his first year of trading:

31/01/2023

(iv) **The date until which he must keep his business records in relation to his first tax year as a trader:**

31/01/2028

(v) **The date of his first payment on account in respect of his income tax and Class 4 national insurance for his second tax year as a trader:**

31/01/2023

(b) (i)

	✓
Four instalments of £6,000 each due on 14 May 2022, 14 August 2022, 14 November 2022 and 14 February 2023 with a balancing payment of £12,000 due on 14 April 2023	
One payment due on 31 January 2024	
Four instalments of £9,000 each due on 14 May 2022, 14 August 2022, 14 November 2022 and 14 February 2023	
One payment due on 1 August 2023	✓

(ii)

	True ✓	False ✓
The maximum penalty for an error in a tax return which is deliberate but not concealed is 75%.		✓ (70%)
If an individual files their 2021/22 tax return online on 13 January 2023, HMRC can start an enquiry at any time before 31 January 2024.		✓ (one year from actual filing date)
If a company files its tax return two months late, the penalty is £100.	✓	

(c) Melton plc will be liable for a penalty of up to £3,000 if it does not retain its records until 31 July 2027 .

(d) £7,179

	£
Income tax £(10,600 – 9,000 payments on account)	1,600
Class 2 NIC	159
Class 4 NIC £(1,800 – 1,350 payments on account)	450
Capital gains tax	4,970
Amount payable on 31 January 2023 for 2021/22	7,179

There are no payments on account for Class 2 NIC or capital gains tax.

The answer £2,050 is just the income tax and the Class 4 NIC. The answer £7,020 ignores the Class 2 NIC. The answer £5,270 treats the Class 2 NIC and the capital gains tax as having payments on account.

(e) A sole trader is required to keep their accounting records for **60** months after the **31 January that follows the end of the tax year**

(f) The minimum % error for an unprompted careless error is 0%. This can be found in the reference material that you have access to in your exam.

Task 9

(a) (i) If Frank operates as a sole trader:

- He will be taxed on the £100,000 profits (subject to any tax adjustments required) regardless of any drawings/ owner's salary that he chooses to take. This is as the business is taxed before any profits are extracted.
- He will have trading income and be subject to income tax as non-savings income. The personal allowance will cover the first £12,570 of this income with the next £37,700 being taxed at 20% and the balance at 40%.
- Frank will also pay Class 2 NIC at £3.05 per week. He will also pay Class 4 NICs on his trade profits in excess of £9,568 at a rate of 9%. Once his profits exceed £50,270 he will pay Class 4 NIC on the excess at only 2%.

If Frank operates as a company:

- The company will pay corporation tax on any profits at 19%.
- The salary of £50,000 taken by Frank together with the employer's NIC thereon will be tax deductible.
- The employer's NIC will be at 13.5% on any salary over £8,840. However, provided Frank is not the only employee of the company, an employment allowance of £4,000 will cover the first £4,000 of employer's NICs.
- Frank will pay employee's NIC on his £50,000 salary. He will pay at 12% on the salary in excess of £9,568.

(ii) If Frank were to take a lower salary and instead extract profits by way of dividend he would be able to take advantage of the lower rates of income tax due on dividends (7.5%/32.5% and 38.1% rather than 20%/40%/45%) and the fact that there is no NIC due on dividends.

This would more than likely outweigh the disadvantage that dividends are not a tax deductible expense for a company.

(b) Tax planning or avoidance is the legal action of taxpayers to minimise their tax liability. HMRC makes a distinction between tax planning – using reliefs as they are intended- and tax avoidance – exploiting loopholes in the law. Tax evasion involves the deliberate suppression of information or providing deliberately false information, and is illegal.

Jim's suggestion is tax evasion.

Tax evasion is punishable by a custodial sentence and/or a fine.

Task 10

(a)

	True ✓	False ✓
Zowie Ltd can set its loss against its total income in the year ended 31 March 2021. • A company must make a current year claim first before it can carry back the trade loss.		✓
Zowie Ltd can set its loss against its total income in the year ended 31 March 2022.	✓	
Zowie Ltd can set its loss against its total income in in the year ended 31 March 2023.	✓	

(b)

	2020/21 £	2021/22 £	2022/23 £
Trading profits	32,000	0	18,000
Trading loss offset against future year	0	0	(12,000)
Property income	6,000	16,000	21,000
Trading loss offset against current year	0	(16,000)	0
Trading loss offset against previous year	(38,000)	0	0
Net income	0	0	27,000

Task 11

(a)

Asset	Market value £	Original cost £	TWDV £	Impact
Factory	323,000	300,000		Chargeable gain
Warehouse	110,000	100,000		Chargeable gain
Plant & machinery	10,000	70,000	5,000	Increase in trading profit
Goodwill	40,000	0		Chargeable gain
Inventory	15,000	17,000		Decrease in trading profit

(b)

Statement	True ✓	False ✓
If Isabella, who owned 100% of the shares in Willis Ltd, had worked for the company and owned the shares for 10 years and Willis Ltd is an investment company, she will qualify for business asset disposal relief giving her a 10% tax rate on her gains. • Investment companies do not qualify for business asset disposal relief.		✓
If Turrell Ltd had ceased to trade on 31 December 2020, the disposal will not qualify for business asset disposal relief. • Provided the shares are sold within 3 years of the company ceasing to trade business asset disposal relief is still available.		✓

(c)

	£
Proceeds	600,000
Less cost	(100,000)
Chargeable gain/allowable loss	500,000
Annual exempt amount	(12,300)
Taxable gain	487,700
CGT @ 10% (Business asset disposal relief)	48,770
Proceeds	600,000
Less CGT	(48,770)
Post-tax proceeds	551,230

Reference material

1 Income tax

Trading allowance			£1,000
Personal allowance			£12,570
	Basic rate (0-£37,700)	Higher rate (£37,701 - £150,000)	Additional rate (Above £150,000)
Salary	20%	40%	45%
Dividends	7.5%	32.5%	38.1%
Trading income	20%	40%	45%

- Income tax computations will not be required in the assessment, but the rates may be used in tax planning discussions.

2 Income tax basis period rules

Ongoing business	Current year basis		
Year of commencement	Actual basis		
	Accounting period <12 months ends in the year	Accounting period ≥12 months ends in the year	No accounting period ends in year
	Tax first 12 months of trade	Tax 12 months to accounting date	Actual basis
Third tax year	Tax 12 months to the accounting date		
Final tax year	Tax from end of basis period in previous tax year to the date of cessation. Deduct overlap profits		

3 National Insurance (NI)

Class 2 contributions	£3.05 per week
Small profits threshold	£6,515
Class 4 contributions on trading profits between £9,568 and £50,270	9%
Class 4 contributions on trading profits above £50,270	2%

- Dividends are not subject to NI
- Salaries are subject to:
  - employee NI at 12% between £9,568 and £50,270 and 2% above £50,270
  - employer NI at 13.8% above £8,840 (an employment allowance of £4,000 is available)
- Calculations of NI on salaries will not be required in the assessment but the rates may be used in tax planning discussions.

4 Capital gains tax

Annual exempt amount	£12,300
Basic rate	10%
Higher rate	20%
Business asset disposal relief rate	10%
Business asset disposal relief lifetime allowance	£1,000,000

5 Corporation tax

Rate of corporation tax	19%

6 Capital allowances

Annual investment allowance	£1,000,000
Writing down allowance – assets other than motor cars	18%
Super deduction – expenditure by companies after 1 April 2021	130%
Writing down allowance cars: – CO2 emissions 0g/km – CO2 emissions up to 50 g/km – CO2 emissions over 50 g/km	 100% 18% 6%
Small pools allowance	£1,000
Structures and buildings allowance	3%

7 Disallowed expenditure

Type of expense	Disallowable in calculation of trading profit	Notes
Fines and penalties	Fines on the business Fines on directors/owners	Employee fines are not disallowed if incurred in the course of their employment.
Donations	Political donations Donations to national charities	Donations to local charities are allowable (these will only be examined for unincorporated
Capital expenditure	Depreciation Loss on disposal Capital items expensed	Capital allowances may be available.

Type of expense	Disallowable in calculation of trading profit	Notes
Legal and professional	Relating to: – capital items – purchase/renewal of a long lease – purchase of a short lease (50 years or less) – breaches of law/regulations.	Legal fees on the renewal of a short lease (50 years or less) are allowable.
Entertaining and gifts	Customer gifts (unless <£50 per annum, not food, drink, tobacco, or cash vouchers and contains business advertising). Customer/supplier entertaining.	Staff gifts and staff entertaining are allowable.
Cars	Depreciation. Private use by owners. 15% of lease cost if leased car >50g/km Co2 emissions.	
Private expenditure of owner (unincorporated businesses only)	Goods taken for own use. Salary of owners. Private use % by owners. Private expenditure, e.g., class 2 and 4 NICs, legal and professional fees for personal expenditure.	Reasonable salaries of family members are allowable.

8 Trading losses

Loss option	Sole trader/Partner	Company
Carry forward	Against future profits of the same trade only. Applies automatically to first available profits. Applies after any other elections or if no elections are made.	Losses not relieved in the current accounting period or previous 12 months are carried forward and an election can be made to set against total profits in future periods.
Current year/carry back	Against total income in the current and/or previous tax year in any order. If opted for in either year, the amount of loss used cannot be restricted to preserve the personal allowance. Make claim by 31 January 2024 for 2021/22 tax year.	Can elect to set trading losses against current accounting period 'total profits'. Qualifying charitable donations will remain unrelieved. If the above election is made, can also carry back trading loss to set against 'total profits' within the previous 12 months. Claim within 2 years of the end of the loss-making period.

Loss option	Sole trader/Partner	Company
Opening year loss relief – loss in first four years of trade	Against total income of the previous three tax years on a FIFO basis. If opted for, losses will be used to reduce total income as much as possible in each year and cannot be restricted to preserve the personal allowance. Make claim by 31 January 2024 for 2021/22 tax year.	N/A
Terminal loss relief	Against trading profits of the previous 3 years on a LIFO basis. Claim within 4 years from the end of the last tax year of trade.	Against total profits of the previous 3 years. Claim within 2 years of the end of the loss-making period.

9 Chargeable gains – Reliefs

Relief	Conditions
Replacement of business assets (Rollover) relief	Available to individuals and companies. Examinable for companies. Qualifying assets (original and replacement) – must be used in a trade and be land and buildings or fixed plant and machinery. Qualifying time period – replacement asset must be purchased between one year before and three years after the sale of the original asset. Partial reinvestment – if only some of the sales proceeds reinvested then the gain taxable is the lower of the full gain and the proceeds not reinvested.
Gift relief (holdover relief)	Available to individuals only. Qualifying assets – assets used in the trade of the donor or the donor's personal company, shares in any unquoted trading company or shares in the donors personal trading company. A personal trading company is one where the donor has at least 5%.
Business asset disposal relief	Available to individuals only. Gain taxable at 10%. £1m lifetime limit For 2021/22 a claim must be made by 31 January 2024. Qualifying assets: – the whole or part of a business carried on by the individual (alone or in partnership). The assets must have been owned for 24 months prior to sale – assets of the individual's or partnership's trading business that has now ceased. The assets must have been owned for 24 months prior to cessation and sale must be within 3 years of cessation – shares in the individual's 'personal trading company' (own at least 5%). The individual must have owned the shares and been an employee of the company for 24 months prior to sale.

10 Payment and administration

	Sole trader/Partners	Company
Filing date	31 October following the end of the tax year if filing a paper return. 31 January following the end of the tax year if filing online. Amendments can be made within 12 months of filing.	Filed on the later of 12 months after end of AP or 3 months after the notice to deliver a tax return has been issued. Company can amend return within 12 months of the filing date.
Payment date	31 January following the end of the tax year. If payments on accounts are due: • first POA – 31 January during tax year • second POA – 31 July after tax year • balancing payment – 31 January after tax year. POA's are each 50% of the previous years income tax and class 4 NICS due by self- assessment. POA's are not required for capital gains or class 2 NICs. POA's are not due if prior year tax payable by self-assessment is less than £1,000 OR if >80% of prior year tax was collected at source.	Small companies (annual profits less than £1.5 million): 9 months + 1 day after end of the accounting period (AP). Large companies (annual profits greater than £1.5 million) must estimate the year's tax liability and pay 25% of the estimate on the 14th day of each of the 7th, 10th, 13th and 16th month from the start of the accounting period.
Interest	Charged daily on late payment	Interest charged daily on late payment. Overpayment of tax receives interest from HMRC. Interest is taxable/tax allowable as interest income.
Penalties for late filing	£100. After 3 months, £10 per day for up to 90 days. After 6 months, 5% tax due (or £300 if greater). After 12 months, 5% tax due (or £300 if greater) if not deliberate. After 12 months, 70% of tax due (or £300 if greater) if deliberate and not concealed. After 12 months, 100% tax due (or £300 if greater) if deliberate and concealed.	£100. After 3 months, £100. After 6 months, 10% of unpaid tax. After 12 months, 10% of unpaid tax.

	Sole trader/Partners	Company
Late payment	30 days late – 5% of tax outstanding at that date. 6 months days late – 5% of tax outstanding at that date. 12 months late – 5% of tax outstanding at that date.	N/A
Notify of chargeability	5 October following the end of the tax year	Within 3 months of starting to trade.
Enquiry	Within 12 months of submission of return. Penalty for failure to produce enquiry documents = £300 + £60 per day.	Within 12 months of submission ofreturn. Penalty for failure to produce enquiry documents: £300 + £60 per day.
Record retention	Five years from filing date. Penalty for failure to keep records is up to £3,000.	Six years after the end of the relevant accounting period. Penalty for failure to keep proper records is up to £3,000.

11 Penalties for incorrect returns

Type of behaviour	Maximum	Unprompted (minimum)	Prompted (minimum)
Careless error and inaccuracy are due to failure to take reasonable care	30%	0%	15%
Deliberate error but not concealed	70%	20%	35%
Deliberate error and concealed	100%	30%	

Notes